THE CONSTITUTION
OF THE
UNITED STATES
OF
BEING

The art of self-love, fulfilling your dreams
and finding joy - no matter what.

BY LISA J. BUTLER

Copyright © 2013 by Lisa J. Butler

Content: Lisa J. Butler
Cover Photo: Andreas Krappweis
Cover Design: Lisa J. Butler & Chris Headford (Wattlegum Webworks)

All rights reserved. No part of this book may be reproduced by any mechanical, photographic or electronic process, or in the form of a phonographic recording, nor may it be stored in a retrieval system, transmitted or otherwise copied for public or private use – other than "fair use" as brief quotations embodied in articles and reviews – without the prior written permission of the publisher.

The author of this book does not dispense medical advice or prescribe the use of any technique as a form of treatment for physical, emotional or medical problems without the advice of a health care professional, either directly or indirectly. The intent of the author is to offer information of a general nature to assist you in your quest for physical, emotional and spiritual health and well-being. In the event you use any of the information in this book for yourself, the author and publisher assume no responsibility for your actions.

ISBN Details:
Trade Paperback: 978-0-9923584-1-9
Kindle E-Book: 978-0-9923584-0-2

DEDICATION

*For Mason,
my gorgeous son who is the light of my life and the source of so much joy in each day. I'm so glad you chose me to be your mother, sweetheart, and I love you more than anyone else in the whole wide world.*

&

*For J,
who taught me through example about humility, strength and resilience, and whose gentle love, support and friendship saved my life more than once. I will love you always.*

constitution [ˌkɒnstɪˈtjuːʃən]
n
1. the act of constituting or state of being constituted
2. the way in which a thing is composed; physical make-up; structure
3. (Government, Politics & Diplomacy) the fundamental political principles on which a state is governed, esp when considered as embodying the rights of the subjects of that state
4. (Government, Politics & Diplomacy) (often capital) (in certain countries, esp Australia and the US) a statute embodying such principles
5. a person's state of health
6. a person's disposition of mind; temperament

Collins English Dictionary – Complete and Unabridged
© *HarperCollins Publishers 1991, 1994, 1998, 2000, 2003*

"A constitution is a set of fundamental principles or established precedents according to which a state or other organization is governed."

The New Oxford American Dictionary, Second Edn.,
Erin McKean (editor), 2051 pages, May 2005, Oxford University Press

STATEMENT 13..146

As you journey along your life's path, don't be afraid to step off it occasionally. There is much beauty to be found on the side of the road, and new experiences to discover. The discoveries on these side journeys will help you further 'down the track'.

Poem: **Your dreams are just a step away**................147

STATEMENT 14..156

At all times, remember to honour and respect your Self. Enjoy your Self and be excited about the life you've been given.

Poem: **You Deserve the Best of Everything**.............157

STATEMENT 15..166

You are both the Clay and the Potter. Delight in your changes, growth and Power.

Poem: **The Power Within**....................................167

STATEMENT 16..175

Remain loving and joyful, for this is the deepest essence of Being.

Poem: **I wish you abundance in all things**..............176

GUIDELINES FOR A SUCCESSFUL LIFE (1998)............184

ACKNOWLEDGEMENTS....................................186

ABOUT THE AUTHOR..188

INTRODUCTION

Just for the record, I'm not a highly enlightened guru-type individual. I'm about as far from 'perfect' as anyone can get and I've done plenty of things in my life that I'm not proud of; things that have caused me to feel great pain, shame and loss, and I know I've caused others pain in the process too. Still, I've always considered myself to be a good person, though I have (and still can) get out-of-control, frustrated and stressed at times. So, before you dive into this book with me, you should know a little about my background and personality, just so you know what you're getting yourself into.

I'm a recovering compulsive overeater with an addiction to sugar and white flour products. My addiction is no different to that of an alcoholic or a drug addict. For me, there is no such thing as being able to have just one biscuit or just one ice cream, or just one extra helping at dinner. Compulsive overeating, binging, and food addiction is real and it's deadly. My favourite food is chocolate, so as you can imagine, it kills me that I can't eat it, but I know it will kill me if I do. Life sucks sometimes.

I'm compulsive in other ways too. I jump into anything I feel good about without always taking stock of the possible consequences. I'm fiery and passionate, and that gets me into hot water at times too. When I give my heart, I give it completely and up until recently I've usually given it to the people who are least likely to love me back. I'm menopausal now, but those who've known me for more than a few years would probably swear I'd been born hormonal and that the condition is a constant and permanent one! Sometimes I'd agree with them.

Depression is something I've suffered with since childhood, though it wasn't really diagnosed until I was in my late 20's. The worst times of depression were through my school years when I was bullied relentlessly and lived a life filled with fear so great that years later I can still feel the utter terror when I think of it.

I attempted suicide when I was seventeen and have seriously contemplated it a number of times since but I only feel that way when I'm very depressed. These days, I don't consider suicide to be a viable option for me. 99% of the time I love my life, and I want to live to become one of those feisty, eccentric old ladies in a big old house with cats perched on the window sills and a rose garden for holding soirees on Sunday afternoons, surrounded by music and interesting creative folk. I intend to eat chocolate on my eightieth birthday.

In my late 20's when I terminated a pregnancy, the depression and overeating hit really badly. It was a frightening and disorienting spiral that drove me close to insanity. I went on anti-depressants for a while but they made me feel numb and I wandered through those many months feeling like a zombie. I live on either end of the emotional spectrum and I'd rather feel really depressed sometimes than feel nothing at all. So, for better or worse, I gave anti-depressants the flick.

Post-natal depression felt like drowning. That was in my late 30's when my beautiful son was born, and it lasted several years. I was in the throes of my food addiction, my relationship with my son's father had broken down, and I felt completely out of control, helpless and alone.

In the past few years, deep depression hit me again when I suffered a business disaster and found myself deeply in debt and on the brink of bankruptcy. I was lucky. By that stage I had begun to discover the truth about my eating issues and had found help to address them. I stopped overeating, stopped consuming sugar and flour products and had more control over my behaviour and emotions. Though still deeply in debt as I write this, I am free of the crippling depression and compulsive overeating that ruled me for so many years, and I feel excited and positive about the next chapter of my life.

I'm a fairly 'matter-of-fact' person in some ways, but I'm a hopeless (hopeful?) dreamer and idealist in many others. I sometimes drive myself (and those around me) crazy, but all in all, I do feel that I've come a long way. I've learned a lot, and I'm proud to be able to say that at least consciously, and perhaps even subconsciously, I'm becoming fearless.

I love wholeheartedly and without reservation. If I love you, it will be forever and I will give you anything you want if it is within my power. My heart rules me. I often wish my head had more of a say but it often loses the argument. Such is my life. Actually, with all the ups and downs, I wouldn't change any of it now. My experiences have created me as I am today - and I like who I've become and who I'm becoming. I'm not afraid of the future anymore.

I like the person I see in the mirror. I'm strong and resilient, and finally, after years of hating myself, I can now admire the survivor I see each morning as I'm applying my makeup. I can frown over a new line developing on my forehead and then smile as I appreciate my perfect imperfection.

There are many great teachers I've learned from along the way but the greatest of these have been the ones closest to me; my parents, my sister, my beautiful beloved friends and even the bullies and abusers over the years, have taught me how to love myself and treat myself and others in a compassionate, respectful and honourable way. I'm still evolving – and I expect that I always will, because that is the very nature of Being-ness. In the meantime, all these experiences have shaped me into a loving mother to my son, an inspiring and motivating coach and mentor to my clients and a capable and positive person to be around. Even if I do say so myself!

So, this is me in a nutshell; loving, passionate, creative and occasionally crazy. You've been warned. ☺

***

I've been a 'Writer', in one form or another, since I could hold a pen. In my early teens I wrote poetry as a release, an escape from the hideous life of fear and bullying. I always loved music so I learned how to play chords on the piano and started writing songs when I was fifteen or sixteen. Writing soothed me through every challenge that life threw at me and through every roadblock I threw up in front of myself. It still does.

In 1998, I was inspired to write a piece I called 'Guidelines for a Successful Life'. I just sat down one day and the words tumbled out like they were being dictated to me. It took twenty minutes to write it – and that included a basic manual edit for spelling, punctuation and grammar. It was a magical experience.

Writing the 'Guidelines' felt like receiving a gift from Spirit. Here was a sort of 'code of conduct', not 'Rules' but statements of profound truth that offered me a path to become a better person. They inspired me to follow my dreams, encouraged me to accept and appreciate the way I interact with myself and others, and regardless of challenges and situations that arise, remain true to myself. I only wish I had done more than merely view the Guidelines with awed wonder back then. Perhaps, if I'd really studied them and worked harder at living according to the advice they gave, I wouldn't have had to go through the pain and self-destruction that I continued to create for myself for many more years.

'Guidelines for a Successful Life' was published in a small New Age magazine in my home town in 1998 and received a nice response, but nothing ever really came of it. I've always liked the premise of it though, so ten years later, in 2008, I shared it with the publishing company I was with at that time, but again, nothing came of it. I'm so glad the Universe/God/All That Is saw a greater vision for the Guidelines.

I was never really happy with the title, and I knew there was more I needed to do but not knowing what that was, I decided to release it to Universal Energy and move on with other things. God doesn't pull any punches with me so I figured that when It was ready to reveal the answer, I'd get the message pretty quickly – and I did – four years later, and fourteen years after I wrote the thing. In 2012, in the space of a few hours and with three separate and unrelated incidents, I was given the answer.

3pm: Waiting for my son to come out of school. I was sitting next to some mothers who were discussing an ailment of a relative when one of them suggested that the sufferer had always had a weak constitution. I remember it clearly because it's not a term used much these days when referring to the human physical condition.

4pm: School Council meeting. During the meeting we were discussing the sudden resignation of a Council member. We had to pull out the School Council's Constitution to look up the procedures we needed to follow.

6pm: World News on TV. I was making dinner and as usual the only news being shared was 'The Bad News' so I headed for the remote control as some US political reporter was droning on. "…the congressman stated that he believed the proposed law was unconstitutional and…".

I hit the 'mute' button with relief. "Huh." I thought. "That was kind of curious." Three times in the past few hours I'd heard the same word repeated and it stuck in my mind. I don't believe in coincidence so wondering what it meant, I finished preparing the meal and sat down with my son to eat.

Later that evening, I was perched at my laptop typing away at a novel I'd started (and am yet to finish). Rummaging around my computer for some information I'd researched, I navigated to the folder on my computer desktop that contains all my poems, articles and other written works, when I accidently clicked on the wrong file and, you guessed it, "Guidelines for a Successful Life" popped up on my screen. I stared at it blankly for about twenty seconds, and then time stood still.

If there's one thing the Source Of All Things excels at, its persistence. It had taken three hits and an upper cut but I finally 'got it'. My 'Guidelines' were like a Constitution; A structure for living life well, a means of lovingly and appropriately managing the combined physical, psychological, emotional and spiritual aspects of myself... a Constitution for the United States of my Being.

I can see that the Constitutional Statements are not about gaining perfection. Trust me, that will never happen, nor should we want it to. Perfection means we stop learning, evolving, expanding. No thanks! I love the visceral, lush fertility of imperfection! The Constitution of the United States of Being is a navigational tool, a means by which we can travel our life's path in safety and with joy regardless of the pot holes and rock falls we encounter along the way.

As well as changing the title from 'Guidelines for a Successful Life' to 'The Constitution of the United States of Being' (throughout the book I refer to it simply as the CUSB), I felt a deep desire to make a few minor changes to the text, mostly with the language used and to clarify a couple of the points. This was an intuitive move, the changes as inspired as when I wrote the original Guidelines fifteen years ago. My understanding of All That Is and How It Works has grown in that time, so when I reread the Guidelines so many years later I could 'feel' a deeper, clearer meaning behind the original wording. Perhaps, in time to come, God will inspire more changes in the wording of the Statements. Perhaps they, like us, are meant to evolve too. After all, most Constitutions undergo review and change from time to time. I have included the original 'Guidelines for a Successful Life' in the back of the book as a reference.

A Constitution contains instructions to follow in order to maintain said Constitution, so to me, it made sense that each Statement in the Constitution of the United States of Being should be the basis for a chapter. By taking a deeper look at what each Statement means and choosing how best to implement it, we can create a life of joy, inner peace and self-love regardless of what the world throws at us.

I love the synchronicity of this Constitution. I love the way that whilst each Statement stands on its own as powerful and thought-provoking, they also blend with each other, mix 'n' match style. Every Statement alludes to at least one other, so used together they can help us create a brilliant and beautiful montage for our lives; a blazing prominent backdrop in a painting titled 'Happy and Successful Life'.

You'll note that throughout the book I refer to God in many different ways; Universal Energy, All That Is, Source Of All Things, God, Spirit, Soul-Self, Divine Self, Universal God Force and a few others. I don't want to be tied to one definition. I've yet to come across a definition that, for me, truly encompasses the sheer magnitude, grace and power of the Eternal Force that drives all things. So I use a variety of terms, but they all mean the same thing. Choose what works for you.

Of course, the implementation choices in this book are mine and based on my life experience, but I like to think they are as inspired by God as the original Guidelines were. You can implement the Constitutional Statements my way, your way, or not at all. The choice is yours – and as Statement #12 suggests, your choice will always be right.

Love, light & blessings,

Lisa xox

THE STATEMENTS OF THE CONSTITUTION OF THE UNITED STATES OF BEING

1. Reach out wholeheartedly for your Goals and Dreams.

2. Have absolute Faith and Trust in yourself.

3. Believe you can have, do and be anything you desire.

4. Develop your Instinct and Intuition.

5. Stand up to your fears – they cannot harm you unless you allow them to.

6. Anger and resentment are the two most negative and destructive emotions – learn to live without them.

7. Be loving and kind to yourself, and you will find it easier to be loving and kind to others.

8. The love, respect and friendship of others is a privilege, not a right.

9. You can make changes in yourself, but you cannot force changes in others.

Life is an adventure so...

Be Bold!
Be Inspired!

Taking the first steps
into the unknown
is challenging and thrilling
- and daunting,
but I know you can do it.

It's your life and
you have the power
to transform it.
You, and you alone
know your heart's desires,
so be persistent.

Fuel your dreams
with action and passion,
then watch with wonder
as the metamorphosis takes place.

When you move forward with purpose,
maintaining a clear focus
and a loving heart,
you will be amazed at how quickly
your intentions
will be transformed
into reality.

So go on - let the adventure begin!

1

Goals and dreams are among the biggest of all the building blocks of Human Being-ness. It's fundamental to our human nature to want more, to have desires and dreams to work toward. It's that greater part of our Self, our Soul-Self, at work, stimulating the urge to constantly expand and create new experiences. Always learning, always growing. The desire to want more, to be more and achieve things is one of the major features of who we are and sets us apart from all other living things on this planet.

I view goals as being quite masculine, pragmatic and 'businesslike' in character and often attached to career, financial or academic achievement. Dreams, on the other hand, are more feminine, creative and emotional in nature. Take finances, for example. The goal may be to build an investment portfolio to secure your financial future, but the country cottage, overseas holiday and time to pursue a long-desired hobby – these are dreams.

Goals get us out of bed in the morning. Even the small goals; getting the kids to school, getting to work on time, paying the bills, doing the grocery shopping within budget – all these small, short-term goals are important because they help us achieve our long term goals of ensuring our children get the education they need and we are earning money so we can live reasonably comfortably. Most of us achieve these small, short-term goals without even thinking about it.

For me, dreams are usually more heartfelt, and point toward things that bring feelings of deep joy, satisfaction, abundance and ease to our spirit; the trip to Bali, the dream home, the perfect relationship, a creative outlet, a career that we love – the basic desire to be happy.

We achieve these wonderful feelings in small ways all the time. We go out to dinner occasionally, buy a new pair of shoes, go to a movie, buy a pretty piece of jewellery, indulge in hobbies and spend time in the garden or play on the beach with the kids. All these activities bring feelings of joy and abundance into our lives. Little dreams lived every day.

We seem to approach big goals and dreams differently. Many people feel their big goals and dreams are impossible and so set them aside without even trying, which can lead to feelings of regret or failure. So why is it that the bigger the dream, the harder it appears to achieve? Why does it feel like we're not moving forward, or getting more of the things we want, to feel true joy and freedom in our lives? Why do so many of those big, dreams and goals seem to go unrealised?

How Big Is Too Big?
Firstly, I believe that we place too much emphasis on size. The only real difference between the goals and dreams we achieve on a daily basis and those we don't attempt is our perception. We perceive the size difference and make that a deciding factor. If we could only look at a big goal and see that, in essence, it's no different to a small one, we wouldn't be afraid to attempt it. A big dream or goal might take more time and patience, but believe me, size doesn't matter. A goal is a goal is a goal.

The only thing stopping you from reaching out for a goal is YOU. The biggest fears in reaching out for goals are fear of the unknown and fear of failing. But the reality is, there is nothing to lose in trying. There really isn't. If there is something you really want to achieve and you feel passionate about it, go for it! Make the decision to at least give it a go.

So, having made the decision to reach out wholeheartedly, what are the steps we need to take in order to achieve our goals and dreams?

Consider the world's most successful people throughout history and the goals and dreams they have achieved: entrepreneurs like Thomas Edison, Bill Gates, Richard Branson, Donald Trump and Kerry Packer, performing artists like Luciano Pavarotti, Madonna, Elton John, and Beyonce, and sports people like Mohammad Ali, Tiger Woods and Serena Williams; all of them highly motivated, and relentless in the pursuit of their goals and dreams.

But what else do all these successful 'dreamers' have in common? What has set them apart and driven them forward as they have reached for their goals? Sure, they have had to learn certain skill sets depending on their field of interest – we all do - but what can we learn from them as we pursue our goals and dreams, and what are the personal traits or tools they have developed and implemented daily that we can use too?

There are the five traits that I perceive all successful people have developed within themselves, and we can cultivate them in order to reach for our goals and dreams too.

Courage
There is a huge difference between having a dream and being willing to take action to achieve it, but I believe that when a dream is borne within us, so too is the capacity to make it happen. Yes, it takes guts to take that first step toward our dream, especially if it's a big one, but just like elite athletes, superstars and successful entrepreneurs, we all have the ability.

moment we get up in the morning until the moment our head hits the pillow at night - it's easy to be distracted in this busy, non-stop, cluttered world we live in.

With so much going on in our busy lives, it's important that we find a way to mentally step away from all of it so we can focus on the task at hand. Sometimes I find this a real challenge and I know that many people do. Over the years I've learned a few tricks.

I only work when my son is not around, ie when he's at school or in bed, or otherwise occupied. Apart from the fact that I can't focus with a child racing around, he deserves my time when we are together. This means that I often work to a tight schedule and time management is important so I can stay focused on my goals. I regularly lock times into my schedule to work on my dreams and goals, in the same way that I lock in meetings, client consultations, writing, family functions, Mason's school activities, music events, and my workshops.

Everything - and I do mean everything - goes into my diary. If you have a day job, put time aside at night after the kids are in bed to work on your goal. You have the right to reach for your goals, so lock in a couple of hours on the weekend too. Your family will survive without you for a couple of hours. Ask for their help to make that 'goal time' happen. After all, achieving your dreams will have wonderful repercussions for them too.

We can't control what happens outside of ourselves, so from time to time I have to move my schedule around to fit in unexpected things. The temptation is to simply replace my goal time, but I've become more protective of it these days because my goals are important to me. Just like any other business in my diary, I move the goal time to somewhere else in my week. I have a rule to never move a goal time more than once. I'm slowly learning that in order to look after me there are times when I have to say "no" to people, and as a born 'people pleaser' that's never easy for me – but I'm getting better at it!

Working from home means that I've had to train my family and friends not to 'pop in' unannounced. It was hard in the beginning (for them and for me). Surely I could 'down sticks' for an hour to have coffee or go to lunch or chat on the phone? After all, I don't have an employer to answer to! Well, yeah, I do. Me! These days they understand so they call me first. They know that if I don't answer it's because I'm working and I'll call them back as soon as I'm able to.

I give myself five minutes to pre-prepare my workspace and myself so I don't 'fiddle' and waste precious time. My compulsive personality tends to get in the way and everything has to be perfect before I start. Sometimes it stops me from starting at all. For some people, this sort of fussing and fiddling is a form of procrastination. Either way, nip it in the bud by having everything ready before your designated block of time begins – and then get to work on your dreams.

Focus is a learned behaviour. But that's a good thing because just like any other skill, it means that anyone can learn how to do it. Train yourself to focus and you'll achieve your dreams and goals that much faster.

Persistence
When you are at Point A and your goal is at Point Z, the only way you're going to reach your goal is by putting one foot in front of the other and working your way through the alphabet! We all know that. But it's not always easy to slog it out day after day, especially when the going gets tough and the end goal seems so far away. Sometimes we feel challenged at every turn and it seems like life is conspiring against us.

When I get knocked down again and again as I reach for a dream, I ask myself a simple question. "Is this pain really worth it?" I imagine myself having already achieved the dream, what it feels like and how much joy it is giving me. If my answer to the question is "Hell Yeah!!!" I pick myself up, dust myself off and resolve to keep going.

Persistence is not the same as stubbornness, though they are related. Persistence is continuing steadily, with purpose in spite of opposition, ie; refusing to give up. Stubbornness is being unreasonably obstinate, ie; refusing to give in. There is flexibility in persistence, whereas stubbornness exudes inflexibility.

When I'm feeling challenged to keep going I take a 'time out' and head for whatever will make me feel good. For me, that includes reading inspirational poetry and biographies, watching music videos of performing artists who inspire me, reading books or watching movies that make me feel good, being with friends who make me laugh, and so on.

Other ways to kick the doldrums and regain inspiration to keep going include walking in nature, playing with your pets, listening to uplifting music, meditating, journaling, and speaking with your mentor, coach, best friend or someone who you know will support and inspire you. Do the things that make you feel good and surround yourself with positive influences. When the 'Emotion Metre' goes up into the positive zone you'll feel strong and inspired again and ready to continue moving forward.

No dream comes easy. As one of the five top traits I see in successful people, persistence, to me, seems like the deal clincher. Without it, 99% of dreams are never achieved. I have affirmations and inspirational quotes around my desk. They help me to keep believing in myself, and to never give up. One of my favourites is by Robert Browning:

"…To dry my eyes and laugh at a fall, and baffled, get up and start again…"

Selective Deafness

An absolute 'MUST HAVE' when you are reaching for your dreams – especially the big ones, is selective deafness. The bigger the dream or goal, the more people (especially the people who love you) will be in your ear telling you it can't be done: you'll be disappointed, they don't want you to be hurt, you've done your best but it's time to 'get a real job', when will you ever learn?, you have to put your family/spouse/children/job first, we can't always have everything we want, you'll never get there so give up before it's too late. Blah, blah, blah. I've heard all these and more.

Of course, the people who love us mean well and they really do want us to succeed in life, but it's often their version of our life they want us to have, not our version. Yes, your family and friends love you and don't want you to get hurt so let them know you appreciate their concern. And yes, if your dream includes a business venture or financial commitment of any kind, it's vitally important to understand all the business and financial aspects of it. I learned that one the hard way.

Selective deafness doesn't mean ignoring good business advice or the genuine love and concern of those around you. But in the end, once you've considered these things, there is only one voice you should truly heed and that's the one that lives in your heart. The voice of your intuition will never lead you astray.

It's YOUR dream and you have to live it on YOUR terms. Yes, LIVE it. No one is going to understand and support you as much as you want them to, so do your homework as much as you can then implement your Selective Deafness and go for it.

My Story

In 2006 a dream was born in me. It was the biggest venture I've ever undertaken and I reached for it fearlessly and wholeheartedly. I decided to organise the Australian Songwriters Conference (a four day event), with no previous

Major Event management experience. Those closest to me were extremely negative. I lived with a constant barrage of pleading, disapproving looks and negative comments. With the exception of my dearest, most trusted friend, no one believed I could do it. They didn't believe in me.

But I believed in me and that's all I needed. I had a lot of struggles along the way. There were sponsorship setbacks, financial problems, issues with venues, speakers and more. I had a small but wonderful group of volunteers to help me during the event, a bookkeeper and a media promotion professional to help, but I still had to do 95% of the organising and pre-event work myself, right down to hand-making the lanyards to save money! But I did it. The ASC was a wonderful event and everything I had dreamed it could be. I was left with a lot of debt, but I ran the event three times until finally, I had to concede. The event wasn't attracting sponsorship dollars and my debt was overwhelming.

The ASC became known as one of the best songwriter events in the world, and I know it will continue again one day when the dollars are there to run it. Who knows? Maybe enough people like you will buy this book to make it a best-seller! Then I can run the ASC with 'our' money! Who needs sponsors? ;-)

The point is, if I'd listened to everyone around me who said I couldn't do it, I would never have reached for my dream and the Australian Songwriters Conference wouldn't exist. But I decided to be brave, I believed in myself and the dream deep within my heart, I focused on the end goal, persisted in my quest regardless of the challenges and implemented Selective Deafness when anyone around me became negative. I did all this without realising it at the time, but I can see it now.

I've worked in the music industry for a number of years as a consultant, career coach and event/workshop presenter, and I'm constantly surrounded by singers, songwriters and musicians who display a deep love for music and a relentless drive and desire to create. Some have the simple goal of performing regularly and earning enough, if not to live on, to at least give them some 'play money' for little luxuries every now and then. Many dream of becoming 'Stars' or writing hit songs. They never stop believing they can do it.

For years, they study their craft, take music lessons and workshops, spend their hard-earned cash on recording songs, buying instruments and sound gear, and spend weekends away from their families to tour second-rate venues and stay in flea-bitten cut-price hotels, often working regular day jobs as well. They receive rejection after rejection from the record labels and music publishers they approach.

Through my coaching and mentoring, I try to instil the five essential traits of successful people into my clients. Courage, self-belief, focus, persistence and selective deafness help them maintain their 100% passionate commitment to their goal of a music career. But I also encourage them to enjoy the journey they are on as they pursue their dreams. Being happy in the moment is, after all, our most fundamental goal.

I think that the power of the dream is the key. If your goal means everything to you, you will achieve it in the end. So don't give up.

Reach out wholeheartedly for your goals and dreams because they are right there waiting, knowing they belong to you.

STATEMENT 2

Have absolute Faith and Trust in yourself.

You are infinite, beautiful and
powerful beyond imagining so...

Trust Yourself

Perfect, even in your imperfection,
you have significance and value in this world.

Learn to release your fear,
trust and have faith in your Self
and your inner wisdom will shine through.

If you could only have the same faith in yourself
that the Universe has in you,
then finally, you would understand
just how precious and perfect you are.

Seek out the self-faith and trust
That lies deep within you
and you will know without a doubt
that nothing you dream of
is beyond your capability.

2

We have not come into this physical reality to be insignificant. Not one of us has. As an Energy or Soul Being, we made the decision to journey into this multi-faceted Human State of Being in order to experience ourselves as more, not less.

If we could strip away the bonds that this physical existence imposes on us, and for just a moment recognise and really feel ourselves as the pure living energy we are, we would understand the true nature of our beauty, power and knowledge. We would understand the absolute connection we have to All That Is. We could never again view ourselves with anything less than complete awe, love, faith and trust for we are, always have been, and always will be, infinite and perfectly imperfect.

Being human adds to us, gives us experiences that allow us the opportunity to be greater, gives rise to the growth and expansion of all things, including our Selves, and provides a platform for the continuation of that evolution. It's why we choose to come into this life, and because we come with a knowing that we are infinite and everlasting, we have nothing to fear. In our Energy/Soul State, we have absolute faith and trust that we can never 'not be'.

As with all the CUSB Statements, this one stands alone but is also intimately intertwined with the others. When we trust and have faith in ourselves, we automatically have a high level of self-love, we listen to our intuition, we enjoy healthy relationships with ourselves as well as others and, as discussed in the first chapter, we develop a fearless ability to reach for our dreams and goals knowing we have everything we need within to achieve them. And so we should. After all, if we can't have faith and trust in ourselves, who can we have faith and trust in? Surely, as the creators of our lives and all we experience, we must also acknowledge faith and trust in our ability to do so.

Faith and trust in our Self should be easy. We are extensions of God, Universal Source Energy, All That Is. Whatever you choose to call it, this powerful magnificence is a part of each one of us. In fact, it is the greatest, highest, of all our States of Being. Such is the brilliance of our Being-ness, that it is our truest nature to trust and have faith in our Self knowing that nothing is by accident, all is well, we can never make a wrong choice and we can never not exist.

If only it were that easy to believe and embrace whilst here in our Human State!

The Birth Of Insecurity
The moment we come into this physical life, something changes in our perspective. From the time of our physical birth until we are old enough to fend for ourselves, we are forced to trust others for our physical wellbeing. Babies have little choice - it's a matter of survival. As we grow into freedom-loving, fearless children with 'minds of our own', we are again encouraged (disciplined) to trust the rules and regulations that our parents, teachers and other 'authorities' lay down for us.

Most of us, at some point in adolescence, acquiesce to the apparent wisdom of other, more 'experienced', authorities and begin to lose our sense of self-trust. Some outwardly rebel against the 'establishment' whilst others withdraw into themselves. Somewhere along the line, many of us forget that we can fly with our own wings. We forget that we are intrinsically perfect, capable and complete. Childhood experiences can erode our natural and inherent sense of faith and trust in ourselves and so I believe this Statement is designed to remind us of our true power, and encourage us to reclaim it.

When we spend a lifetime conforming to what others want from us, we can sometimes find ourselves on the slippery slide of 'people pleasing', and doing/being what society expects of us. Suddenly, the expectations of others and what we have attained externally (physically), becomes important to our well-being; the car we drive, the friends we have, the house we live in, the money we make and the partner we choose, all become symbols of our ability to be acceptable, to be worthy.

One of the notable results of our learned dependence on others for our sense of security is that we become more susceptible to feelings of deep hurt and loss. Why? Because anything that exists outside of our Self can be taken away.

We can tend to depend on others to be the catalyst to bolster our self-esteem and self-worth. What others think of us and how much they trust and have faith in us, becomes our motivation to have trust and faith in ourselves. If their esteem, trust or faith in us wanes for whatever reason, or they leave our life, it is like having our sense of Self yanked out by the roots. The effect can be devastating.

This is something I have experienced a number of times over the years. I've unconsciously placed my self-worth in the hands of others I trusted and had faith in because they seemed to feel that way about me – and often they did. And it's great to feel that connection with someone or something that makes us feel good. But with no self-worth of my own, I became an 'energy vampire', sucking the love, esteem, trust, faith and friendship out of them until they had to walk away to save themselves. Without a foundation of trust and faith in myself, I had no firm roots of my own with which to grow and thrive, so I relied on others to provide it and when they couldn't (or wouldn't), I'd lose them, and I'd feel like a little piece of me would die each time.

That's why having absolute faith and trust in your Self is essential. No one can love you, make decisions for you or take care of you as effectively as you can. There is no physical thing, circumstance or person in your life that is permanent, so why base your self-esteem, self-worth or your entire sense of well-being - on the regard you receive from them?

Don't define yourself by your external possessions and influences. They can disappear; leaving you lost and devoid of Self. Be defined by your internal attributes. Learn to take humble pride in ownership of yourself knowing you are whole, complete and self-sufficient. People, possessions, status - all these can leave your life, but you never can.

Trusting and having faith in ourselves leads to healthier, more balanced relationships because we no longer place the burden of our worth or security onto others. Self-trust and –faith means that even when our outer circumstances change, we feel secure and able to continue on with confidence, knowing that all is well. And it means we can enjoy the people and things that come into our life without attachment to, or dependence on, them for our well-being. We can be confident in the decisions we make and the directions we choose to take in life. We don't need the approval of others to feel good about ourselves. Having absolute faith and trust in ourselves gives us the ability to fly with our own wings.

Oh Ye of Little (Self) Faith!
Much like self-belief, faith and trust in the Self can be recovered and nurtured because they are part of our true nature. I believe that even when we think we have no reason to have faith in ourselves, the ability to activate and cultivate it is inherent within us. All we really need is the willingness to believe it exists and the desire to seek it from the inside out.

If you have self-esteem issues (and let's be honest, many of us do), this can be a true exercise in 'believe it until you see it' – the ultimate exercise in faith! I promise you though, the Energy/Soul/God State of your Being knows, with absolute clarity and understanding, that it has faith in itself. And as your Energy/Soul/God State is a fundamental part of YOU, so too is that knowledge of self-faith, whether your Physical and Intellectual States are aware of it or not.

The big question is: How do we, in our Human-ness, experience that knowledge of faith and trust in our Self when society has been chipping away at it for so long? Where do we even begin to start? I don't know that I have a definitive answer to these questions. It's taken me many years to get to a point where I feel confident enough – most of the time - to trust and have faith in myself. For me, this means being able to take care of myself and my needs and those of my young son, being confident in my choices, and letting go feelings of insecurity and fear.

The most helpful factor has been in believing that I was born with Self-trust and -faith built in, even if I've temporarily 'forgotten' it. Every experience allows me the opportunity to exercise my ability to trust and have faith in my Self just a little bit more. It's a slow and incremental process and perhaps one that is continuous, never-ending.

Sharing my life experiences and my thoughts on the Constitution of the United States of Being through this book (actually, sharing the CUSB at all) is definitely an exercise of faith and trust in my ability to withstand the possible rejection, dissent, and even outrage of readers. Mental illness, abortion, suicide, addiction, the belief that there are no wrong choices, that we are God, – I seem to be setting myself up for a lot of opposition. If I could write this book without offending anyone, I would. I'm the queen of 'people pleasing' and I loathe and fear confrontation. But I have to write this book as I'm compelled to; just as the CUSB was written through me, not by me, so too is much of the content of this book driven by my Soul State rather than my Intellectual State.

I'm writing this book to honour and share the beauty and sincerity of the CUSB and to inspire and give hope to readers that our life has the capacity to be great, and that truly, all is well. I'm writing to share that no matter the past or current circumstances, in living by the Statements of the CUSB, we can experience abundance, joy and freedom every day, because it's a choice we make and we can trust in our ability to make it.

Even knowing my pure and noble reasons for writing this book, I will still need to attain a high level of trust and faith in myself and in the Universe in order to send it to print. I guess if you're reading this, I found it! Perhaps that's the secret of this Statement; as primarily spiritual/energy Beings, absolute faith and trust in ourselves has to be equal to having absolute faith and trust in God/Source/Universal Energy. I believe that each one of us is a unique and infinite piece of God, which means we have access to the limitless power of the Universe. You gotta trust that!

Flexing our Self-Trust Muscles
Trusting that we can take care of ourselves - that we are competent, strong and complete in every way – isn't that the outcome we most desire? The capacity really does exist within each one of us to achieve this level of self-sufficiency and assuredness. We know it because we've all had moments of feeling that way from time to time. Like every skill we want to master, we need to consciously practice it. The more we believe self-trust is inside us, and work to develop it, the stronger it will become; like exercising our muscles, the more we use them, the stronger they get.

A great way to flex our self-trust muscles is to consider the ways in which we already feel confident in taking care of ourselves. For example, perhaps you regularly cook healthy and delicious meals for yourself or you're a really good driver. Maybe you're great at maintaining a budget, feel capable at your job, are fantastic at organising your time and tasks, or you are a kind and trusted confidante. There are so many ways we can feel pride and satisfaction with our abilities and the every-day choices we make, but we rarely stop to appreciate them. We don't value or acknowledge satisfaction for our daily accomplishments. But we should, because from this satisfaction is born self-trust. If we start thinking about all our accomplishments from this point of view, we will discover and develop a level of self-trust we could never have imagined.

You have the right to feel proud of your ability to trust and have faith in yourself. It's not about arrogance. You can feel proud and be humble about it at the same time. This isn't about 'tooting your horn' to the world about how competent, strong and complete you are. It's about acknowledging it to your Self. It doesn't matter if other people see these attributes in you (or not); it only matters that YOU do.

We can choose to trust and have faith in our inherent perfection, completeness and infinite-ness or we can reject it. This Statement encourages us to embrace it, wear it like an invisible skin; revel in it. Just thinking about it makes me feel good! Self-faith and -trust is so intrinsic to our well-being that to ignore it or push it away seems arrogant, ignorant and even downright rude - like refusing a beautiful gift that's offered lovingly.

Which, of course, it is.

The Constitution of the United States of Being

STATEMENT 3

Believe you can have, do and be anything you desire.

You can achieve anything...

The Universe is abundant
with everything you desire for yourself.
You really can make your dreams come true
if you believe in them enough.

Sometimes, the hardest thing to do
is know we are worthy
of the things we most desire.
I want you to know that you really do deserve
all the wonderful dreams you have.

All you need to do
is ask for what you want,
and everything your heart desires
will come to you.

Focus on your goals
and the good feelings you have
when you imagine achieving them.
Live in a state of appreciation and love,
then let go and allow yourself
to receive the abundance
you so richly deserve.

Don't give up on your dreams.

3

Often, when I make this Statement to people, they disagree with me. If a person has no legs they can't run a four-minute mile no matter how much they might desire it.

I believe this Statement is pointing toward the principles of the Law of Attraction. When I wrote the original 'Guidelines for a successful Life', the precursor to the Constitution of the United States of Being, this Statement read; 'You can have, do, be anything you desire – if you desire it enough.' I admit that I didn't believe this Statement either. After all, how many times had I begged God for enough money so that I could pay basic bills - and not received it? How often had I requested a beautiful, loving relationship but received the opposite? And, how often had I pleaded to be happy and gone from miserable to suicidal instead? Lots! But I've discovered something astounding.

The truth is, The Universal Force has always given me exactly what I wanted, I just didn't realise it at the time.

Once I gained a greater knowledge of the Law of Attraction and the truth underlying this Constitutional Statement, I also understood my imperfect interpretation of it. Yes, we CAN have anything we desire. If fact, we are meant to have all that we ask for. That's the basis of the Law of Attraction. But desire on its own is not the key to getting what we want; nor is action. These are the first steps, but once we ask for something, we have to take a mental step back from it to let the Universe to do its job, and then allow ourselves to receive what we've asked for. And there's the challenge.

Stop Trying So Hard
We have a tendency to get in the way of our dreams. We really do. We ask for stuff and then we keep asking for it, and asking, and asking and asking. Sheeesh! At some point we have to stop asking so the Universe can actually deliver. We have to let go, release, and allow the next step in the process.

According to Abraham (www.abraham-hicks.com), there are three steps to the Law Of Attraction process. Step one is to ask (this is our step and we do this all the time – we are actually really good at this step). Step two is not our step. This is where The Universe delivers our request (every single time without fail). Step three is our step again: to allow ourselves to receive the thing we asked for that the Universe has so graciously delivered. This is the step where, for most people, it all seems to fall apart. Here's a parallel;

Step One: You pick up the phone and call Mr Jones at Jones' Hardware Store with a shopping list and you ask for the goods to be delivered. You hang up the phone fully expecting the goods to arrive.

Step Two: A little while later there is a knock on the door. "Delivery from Jones' Hardware Store" the delivery man calls out.

Step Three: You open the door to receive the goods.

Of course, if you don't open the door, the goods can't be delivered. They'll sit at the store waiting for you to either pick them up or answer the door next time you ask for them to be delivered. Simple.

So why is it so hard to open that damn door?!

It's interesting that while writing this chapter I have experienced exactly the type of situation where I've used Law of Attraction to make something happen and then almost blown Step Three. God's timing is always perfect!

I had been close to cancelling a road trip to visit friends because it was right after Christmas, money was tight and my son, who was on school holidays, wanted to do some fun things with me. I didn't know how I was going to find the money to buy groceries, let alone go on the trip. I felt I couldn't do both. I emailed my past and present clients letting them know the dates I was available for coaching sessions through the holidays in the hope of bringing in some extra, much-needed funds, but clients always drop off the radar over December and January. They need holidays too. I really wanted to go on the trip but didn't know how I could make it happen with no clients booked in.

A few days before I was going to call my friends to cancel, my mother came over for coffee and offered to pay for the trip so I could go and relax with my friends. She knew how much it meant to me and that I was struggling financially. Because of my conditioning, I shrank inside. I felt I couldn't accept her offer because a) I felt guilty taking it to indulge in a pleasure – after all, the trip was a 'want' not a 'need', and b) I wanted to be able to look after myself and not keep accepting help from my parents. I felt I didn't deserve to go if I couldn't make it happen myself. I thanked her for her lovely offer but declined. We talked about why I didn't want to accept her gift and she asked me to think about it some more and that the offer was still there for me should I change my mind.

Over the rest of that day and evening I realised that this situation was the perfect opportunity for me to change a pattern of only accepting help when I really needed it. I did deserve a break away and my mother was offering me a gift with only the most loving of intentions. So was God; after all, I had asked for the money to go on the trip. But I had to stop constantly attaching self-imposed conditions to receiving my requests and allow myself to accept them in whatever way the Universe chose to deliver them. I called my mother and accepted her gift in the spirit with which it was given. And I had a fantastic, relaxing, inspiring week with my friends.

Where's Your Focus?
If you want financial abundance in your life but all you think about is the lack of money in your current situation, then you'll get more lack, not more money. If you want a beautiful loving relationship but all you think about is your fear of landing yourself in another terrible relationship, you are focusing on your fear and your past terrible relationship and will be sent more of the same. And if you want to be happy but your focus is on how miserable you feel, guess what?

Focusing on what we want (not on what we don't want) is important, but it's also essential to be in a positive emotional place. We can do this by retraining our thoughts to be focused on feeling good on a daily basis. Appreciation in our daily lives allows us to feel good in the moment. It helps us feel fulfilled without even having received what we've asked for yet.

How much easier is it to walk through an open door than it is to walk through a closed one? Think about the Law of Attraction in the same way. If you are living in a positive, appreciative and happy emotional state it is much easier for All That Is to deliver your request for more of that, than if you are in a negative, unsatisfied, unhappy emotional state.

Appreciating the great stuff in our life attracts more great stuff! OMG! How easy is that!

Raising Self-Esteem To Get What You Want
It's easy to say on a conscious level "*Yes, I want that.*" But if, at a subconscious or even cellular level, your underlying belief is that you don't really deserve it or it's impossible or it's never going to happen, that's your real focus, your truest belief, and

that's what you will draw to yourself. Law of Attraction always mirrors your truest belief.

So, what if you want to run a four minute mile and you have no legs? My question to you would be "Which feeling flows through you when you think about trying – doubt or anticipation?"

If you are feeling electric anticipation – you know you can do it and you will. Way cool! With the use of modern sports prosthetics, elite amputee athletes are already achieving amazing speed that rivals able-bodied athletes, so there's no reason why you shouldn't get out there and work toward your dream.

If doubt underlines your feelings, perhaps you need to look at why the challenge is important to you. What is compelling you to want it so much? Is it really about challenging yourself physically and mentally or is it more to do with proving your worth to yourself or others?

The desire to prove one's worth stems from a lack of self-esteem and the belief that somehow you're not good enough, so you need to address that first. How can you possibly succeed when, at your core, you don't think you're good enough or worthy of finding success in your life?

Addressing self-esteem issues can take time – after all, they didn't just turn up in a rain shower! They may have been developing for many years and been caused by trauma or negative input from others as a child. Here are my tips to developing a healthy self-esteem and feelings of self-worth:

- Go easy on yourself. You deserve your love, not your derision.

- Spend time with people who are happy and positive and avoid those who make you feel bad.

- See a counsellor or psychologist. We all can use a little analysis at times!

- Try Hypnotherapy as a means of rewriting your subconscious thoughts and establishing positive feelings about yourself and your life.

- Do regular volunteer work. Giving service to others without expectation of a reward is a great way to feel genuinely good about your Self.
- Buy yourself a bunch of flowers to say I love you to YOU! It might sound silly, especially if you're a guy, but give it a go because it really works! Romance yourself!

- Spend time in nature, walking, fishing, bird watching – or just sitting quietly. Take in the healing, nurturing energy of a forest, the ocean, an open plain or a beautiful garden.

- Be with children. Kids are authentic, and their sense of freedom, fun and playfulness is delightful and entertaining to be around.

All these pastimes can make you feel good - about your Self, the world around you and life in general. When you do things that make you feel good, and you do this consistently, over time you literally change the way your brain processes information and the result is the transformation of your physical and emotional responses from negative to positive.

What you focus on is what you get, so focus on whatever makes you feel happy, appreciative, positive and empowered and it won't take long for this conscious moment by moment practice to become natural and lifelong.

(im) Possible Dreams

So, let's return to that pesky implausible impossible dream the Universe has thrown at us, of being able to have, be and do anything we desire. It's looking little more likely now, isn't it?

Okay, I admit that there are some circumstances where we want something in particular but we know it's more than a stretch.

Take this wild example: If you're a forty year old sales rep with a high school education, wife, three kids and a mortgage, and you want to be an astronaut, you're probably staring down the barrel of some pretty serious disappointment. But it doesn't mean you should just shove the dream under the rug and forget about it. You can still indulge in your passion for space and aeronautics.

Contact your nearest observatory and find out about tours, volunteering and local interest groups. Read books and watch documentaries on space and space travel. Get online and look for chat rooms and forums specifically for space enthusiasts. Have you visited the NASA website? It's AMAZING!

OMG! What about saving up for a once-in-a-lifetime trip to NASA in Houston or Florida? They have fantastic tour experiences – you can even have lunch with the astronauts! You could time it with a mission launch and be there for the big event. I'm excited just thinking about it and I have no desire to be an astronaut!

You might think this is all a little ridiculous, that I'm speaking as someone who doesn't understand the deep desire to make an impossible dream come true. The fact is I did have a big dream that I didn't reach, and it hurt like hell.

My Story
As a teen I loved to sing. My mother was a singer in club bands and I wanted to be just like her – beautiful, talented, graceful, adored by her audiences, and loved and respected in the community. I wanted to travel the world and sing in the great arenas to thousands of screaming fans.

When I was old enough, I sang locally from time to time in clubs and bars and although I always got a good reception, usually some drunken moron would sidle up to me afterwards to tell me what a great voice I had and if I could just lose some weight I could go places. Oh, and this little gem, straight to my face "Great voice, nice face - shame about the rest of you." Nice. Like I didn't hate myself enough, I'd just go home and eat more.

I paid big money (for me) to learn with a company that produced advertising jingles for TV and radio. They were sharks and I learned pretty quickly the tricks they used in the studio to make you sound good (or bad if they wanted to stretch out the learning process to get more money out of their hapless 'students'). I wrote songs and had a couple recorded in local studios, but by the time I was in my mid-twenties, I 'knew' it wasn't going to happen. Having a great voice wasn't enough. I didn't have the personal strength or the necessary music business knowledge, contacts and networking skills to achieve my dream at that time in my life. Mostly, I realise now that I didn't really believe in myself or that I was worthy of my dream. So although I was consciously begging for what I wanted (to be a successful touring and recording artist) I was unconsciously expecting disappointment and failure, and as that was my true underlying belief, the Universe delivered.

I kept writing and playing music on the piano at home though, and somewhere along the line it occurred to me that I could still indulge in my passion by working inside the music industry. That's when the song writing bug really hit, and I loved it. It allowed me to be in the industry, spend time with talented and creative people, and be surrounded with music.

There was no professional industry assistance (that I was aware of) when I was young. Perhaps that's why running the Australian Songwriters Conference years later was so important to me. I wanted to help others achieve their music dream in a way that was never available to me. This also rings true of my coaching and mentoring. I began having sessions with a professional coach when I started organising the first ASC. I loved the idea of motivating and inspiring others in this way so I completed a coaching course and have been helping people achieve their dreams ever since.

I still sing around the house and in the car. I even have a weekly singing lesson with my mother who is now a professional singing teacher, and I indulge in a little karaoke fun from time to time because I love to sing. I'm happy and fulfilled with what I do and I managed to hold onto my real dream – to use my skills, knowledge and love of music to help others along their path.

I have learned over the past few years that we really can have, do and be anything, and we always get what we ask for. Always. The key is to focus on appreciation, feeling good and thinking about what you want (as opposed to what you don't want), and everything you dream of in life will truly be made available to you.

STATEMENT 4

Develop your Instinct and Intuition.

Let your intuition guide you...

There is a seed of knowing inside you
It is your inner voice,
and it will never lead you astray.
It is the expression of God-knowledge within.

Release the noise and clamour
of life around you
and seek out silent serenity.
Listen to your feelings.
They deliver the vibration of instinct
and the voice of intuition
to sound clearly in your heart.

There is a time to let go
and a time to stand firm,
so be true to yourself and
let your feelings be a belltower,
ringing the inner-wisdom and truth
within your soul.

No matter where you are
or what the circumstances may be,
allow your intuition to guide you
and your choices will always be blessed.

4

As a victim of bullying right through school, instinct was something I relied on pretty heavily to get out of harm's way, though I was often physically overpowered and so I copped the beating anyway. We all possess instinct and intuition but most of us don't tend to cultivate either very much. I didn't begin to cultivate or 'tune in' to my intuition until I was much older, and I still haven't completely learned to trust it, though I'm trying. Yet using these senses can enrich our experience of life one thousand-fold.

For me, instinct is a physical knowing. It alerts us to danger or changes in the atmosphere around us; instinct is what makes our hair stand on end and the adrenaline flow when our body anticipates a fight or flight situation. It also directs us when taking split-second decisive actions in our daily lives. Instinct is primal, masculine and physical in nature.

> *Have you ever been to a night club and suddenly sensed a charge of negative or aggressive energy that made your hair stand on end - just before a fight breaks out?*

Intuition is different, it's more internal. I believe it is a knowing that comes from our super-conscious or Divine Self – that aspect of us that is God. Intuition is born within our Soul, felt through our emotions and is non-physical, feminine and energetic in nature. Whilst it is commonly known as the 'sixth sense', I believe that, as we originally come from the non-physical, intuition is actually our very first sense, and though for many of us it is latent, it is the most significant and essential of all our senses.

> *Have you ever started out to work in the car and suddenly taken a different route than usual, only to discover when you arrived at work that there had been an accident/burst water main/other unforeseen delay on your usual route?*

Trusting our Internal Barometer
Together, instinct and intuition create a very reliable internal barometer for the health and wellness of our United States of Being but we have to remind ourselves to use them, to trust them. How often do you ignore your 'gut' feelings and make decisions or choices that ultimately lead you astray? (Okay, so I know that we can never really be led astray, that each choice is perfect etc, but you know what I mean); your instinct or intuition sends you a signal, you don't go with it and as a result, you find yourself in a situation you'd rather not be in.

Why don't we consistently trust these most basic physiological and soul-deep feelings? What are we afraid of? Perhaps it has something to do with our society's need to 'see to believe'. Perhaps it's only real if there is physical evidence of it. But, isn't that prickling of the skin, sinking feeling in the stomach and rush of energy through our body, excellent physical evidence?

Not if others can't feel it too, says the brain

> *"My spouse will think I'm crazy if I refuse to get in the car this morning because I've got a 'bad' feeling about travelling today".*

Not if it means taking a risk, reasons the brain again;

"This job applicant feels so right for me and my business and I'd really love to employ them, but they don't have all the necessary skills. I should hire someone I don't have to train".

Not when a professional tells you otherwise, insists the brain, against our better judgement...

My Story
One of my most profound experiences with instinct and intuition happened when my son was born. I knew I was having a boy (no intuition needed– the ultrasound scans told the story there!) and I was really excited about welcoming my son into the world, but around the sixth month I began to feel unwell. My pregnancy, up to that point, had been great but I began to blow up like a balloon and my blood pressure, always a little on the low side, began to climb. I look at photos of me at that point and I'm aghast that no one else noticed, or was alarmed by, the red, swollen and sick looking woman in front of them. Perhaps it was a case of familiarity, like the frog that's placed in cold water on a stove and slowly boiled to death, ignorant of the changing temperature until it's too late.

I knew something was wrong and I was worried about pre-eclampsia (toxaemia) because of my age - I was 37 years old - so I went to the doctor and explained my concerns. He told me I was reading too many books and scaring myself and that my blood pressure was 'up' but I was doing fine.

Although I'd terminated a pregnancy years earlier, it had been very early in the pregnancy (around the 6th week), so this was my first real experience with pregnancy and childbirth. I had nothing to compare this experience with, so I chose to ignore my intuition and instincts and listened to the doctor. After all, he was the expert, right?

My son stopped moving inside me about a month later. There are no words to describe the fear and distress. Perhaps it's a feeling that only women who go through this can relate to. I went back to the doctor who suggested I have another scan to assess the situation. And then he told me the scan would cost $130. This doesn't sound like a lot of money, but we didn't have any. I wasn't able to work by that stage, and my partner wasn't working either. We were subsisting on government payments and we didn't have health insurance. Medicare would only cover two scans and I'd had those already as was the norm for a pregnant woman in my age group.

This would have been a good time to know that if I'd gone straight to the hospital casualty section, I would have been taken in and the tests would have been done under my government Health Care Card. But I didn't know and no one told me.

I could have called my mother for the money, but by that stage I was feeling so strung out emotionally that I couldn't think straight. I decided to wait for 24 hours. That night I felt movement again. About six weeks before my due date I couldn't bear the discomfort and sick feeling any longer. I went back to the doctor and my blood pressure was through the roof. This time he did suggest I go straight to the hospital for assessment.

I was diagnosed with pre-eclampsia and the scans showed that my baby had no amniotic fluid around him and he had stopped growing at around 30 weeks. Both my baby and I were now at risk and we would lose him (and maybe me too) if he wasn't delivered immediately. I was raced by ambulance from my local suburban hospital to the big city hospital 90 minutes away. 'Immediately' turned out to be 36 hours later because I had to be pumped full of blood pressure meds and steroids in an attempt to keep me from getting sicker and to force the baby's lungs to develop and strengthen a little before the birth. I was poked, prodded, stuck with needles, discussed at length by doctors as though I wasn't even in the room, and frankly, I was in a daze.

But here's the thing. I wasn't afraid for myself or my baby. As I lay in the ambulance on the way to the city hospital I suddenly knew deep down inside me, with every fibre of my being, that we would both be fine. I was anxious of course. I'd never spent time in hospital and I'd never had a baby, let alone one whose life was in danger. On top of all that, the world was holding its breath as the United States of America went to war in Iraq. It was a completely foreign and disorienting experience for me. But I knew intuitively and instinctually that all would be well. And it was.

Mason was born via emergency Caesarean Section on the evening of 21st March 2003. He didn't even need oxygen. At just 3 pounds 11 ounces, he was tiny - skin over bone - but he was alive and I could tell that it was his intention to stick around and experience this physical State of Being for the blessing it is. He was in the hospital's Special Care Unit for about seven weeks until he had grown enough to take home, and he has grown – into a happy, healthy, compassionate and hilariously funny young man.

I'm not saying that the worst couldn't have happened. Of course it could have – and as I initially chose to ignore my internal barometer, it almost did. Fortunately, I eventually did listen to and trust my intuition (felt in my heart and emotions) and my instincts (felt in my body) and this gave me peace of mind when everything seemed to be going wrong. That trust held me together and helped me through the experience.

Build your Listening Skills
The more we listen, trust and utilise our instincts and intuition, the stronger they become. I think that's the key. Like so many of our personal practices, the more we do it the better we get. Listening to our intuition and instincts and

acting on them on a regular basis, makes our natural internal barometers strong as steel. When we ignore our barometer, we do so at our peril because its function is to guide us toward actions, decisions and situations that will have desirable outcomes for us.

I think that's why this Statement exists in the Constitution. Our instinct and intuition are generated from both our physical and non-physical nature – the basis of our United States of Being – and so are crucial to every aspect of our health, happiness and wellbeing.

Learning to listen closely to our instincts and intuition is really about focus, I think. We all have this internal barometer, but we are constantly bombarded by external stimuli that distract us. How do we redirect our focus internally in a world full of busyness, responsibilities and diversions?

For me, it's about making time each day to be quiet, relaxed and meditative. Having 'alone time' to do this is not always easy, but tuning in to my Self and consciously allowing my mind, body and spirit to 'float downstream' is absolutely essential to my overall health and well-being.

I have a few different means of letting go of external noise;

- meditation and deep breathing exercises

- listening to inspirational, acoustic or classical music

- taking time to be physically still and relaxed with my eyes closed and being aware of surrounding sounds and activity.

These are all ways that I recover my inner focus. I find that when I do these things regularly, my entire Being is refreshed, at peace and completely tuned in to the Self. Not only are my instincts and intuition active and healthy, but I trust them (me) more and I'm more likely to act on my internal barometer rather than against it.

Fear is the greatest barrier we have to making the most of our intuition and instinct. Fear makes us 'second guess' ourselves and stops us from trusting that first thought/feeling that our internal barometer offers. Yet, there is no other aspect of our Self that is as dependable and trustworthy because as part of the perfect Universal/God energy that is within us, intuition and instinct are energetic connections between the physical and non-physical; they are our God-Self talking.

Intuition and instinct will always lead us toward the things we want; positive and joyful decisions and outcomes, trust and confidence in ourselves and in life. When we listen to our internal barometer and act in accordance with it, we step out of our self-imposed boundaries with love and trust knowing that we are steering in the right direction, even if we don't always know where the journey is taking us.

And that's why it's important to nurture this aspect of our Self. Instinct and intuition play a fundamental role in helping us to maintain our sense of joy, security and empowerment. They are like a compass that will always point toward that which our highest Self knows is best for us.

STATEMENT 5

Stand up to your fears – they cannot harm you unless you allow them to.

Embrace the Lion within

The things you fear most are just illusions.
They have no hold over you
save those you give power to...

You are eternal,
there is always enough
of everything you need,
and all your dreams are waiting for you.
Let go of your fears
and allow yourself to shine.

God resides within you
and the courage of a lion
dwells in your heart,
so release your fear
because you are infinite
and everlasting.
No harm can ever truly come to you.

There is nothing to fear
because you are supported
by the Universe.
Embrace the wisdom,
power and love of God
that lies within
and your courage will sustain you
on your joyful journey.

5

This is a big issue for most of us. Some people experience fear so strongly that it completely debilitates them. I know that feeling. Fear creates physical illness and dis-ease, emotional paralysis and spiritual bereavement. So, what is fear? How is it, that this emotion can manipulate us so absolutely? Can we control it or even release it entirely so it doesn't rule (or ruin) our life?

Here's what I think. Somewhere along the line, human beings began to misinterpret the emotion of fear. Tens of thousands of years ago, humans, like other animals, developed instinct as an 'early warning system' for physical danger. They learned that smoke could mean a bushfire, sabre-toothed tigers did not make good cave pets, and some plants were poisonous if eaten. As humans realised that there could be dire consequences to the choices they made in reaction to the world around them, they developed the emotion of fear as a means of avoiding death or injury. It was a logical, healthy and practical response to real physical danger.

Fear is a learned response. We are not born with fear built in, any more than we are born with anger, jealousy, guilt or worry. These are emotions we develop – they are not genetic predispositions. However, I do believe that we are born with the knowledge of the beauty and perfection of the Universe within us, and as such we move from spirit into this physical state, understanding and sensing our absolute well-being. It's what happens to us from the point of birth, and how we react to our experiences, that determines the contents of our emotional 'tool kit' and the effective use of our early warning system.

So, from this viewpoint, the feeling of fear merely prompts us to look carefully at what is causing this acute negative emotion so we can alter our current direction, choice or thought process to promote a more positive outcome. Fear, like any negative emotion, is our Higher Self telling us that we're not happy with the situation and we need to change it. That's it. As an early warning system, that is all fear was designed to do. It was never meant to rule our lives or become a force so great that it should develop into a catalyst for depression, powerlessness and anxiety – nor should it become an excuse for the bad behaviour we witness on the evening news as people cause damage to each other because of their fears – and fear is always the root cause of such behaviour.

So, how do we overcome our fear of fear and return it to its rightful place of 'early warning system'?

Horror Movie Right There On My TV
Be selective about the information you receive from the media. I avoid TV news and current affairs programs, tabloid press, talk back radio and reality shows that televise people behaving at their worst. Iconic Australian rock band, Skyhooks, got it soooo right with their 1975 hit, 'Horror Movie'. All these shows are designed to make us gasp with horror and feel bad about the world and the people we share it with. But the world is actually an amazing place and the reality is, most of the events that happen around us are really wonderful. Most of the people we share our planet with are truly loving, kind and wonderful too. The truth is, the good news far outweighs the bad and yet the good news rarely gets shared. Why is the media determined to fuel fear by only sharing the horror stories (or building a story to horror proportions)? What is the benefit of that? I don't know what

the reasoning is, but I won't buy into it.

I believe we get what we focus on, so why would I want to focus my attention on negative, fear-inducing information?

I remember meeting a woman, several years ago at a music event, who liked watching police and crime shows on TV. When I say 'liked', that's an understatement. Obsession would probably be a more accurate description. In fact, the only shows she watched, without exception, were the ones that related to crime and criminal activities. Reality shows, dramas, movies and documentaries; her entire viewing 'pleasure' lay with this genre.

I was staggered when she told me but kept a straight face and asked her why she was only interested in crime shows. Her answer was that she was afraid of being robbed, or worse, so by watching those programs she could learn how to protect herself against the bad guys. Huh??!! I've got to say that I didn't enter into a discussion with her about it and I've always wondered what happened to her. This woman was filled with fear over something she was worried might happen and was unconsciously choosing to fuel her fear by focusing her attention on more of the same. I'm only guessing here, but the outcome of intense focus has become so obvious to me, I'd be willing to bet that, assuming the woman still focuses her attention in this way, she has been, or will be, the victim of the criminal activity she so desperately wants to avoid.

It's one thing to lock the door at night and have the mail collected when you go on a holiday. Sure, we secure the car when we go shopping, hold onto our handbag or wallet properly and teach our kids about 'stranger danger'. Safe behaviour is just common sense. But when our behaviour is dominated by fear and "What ifs?" our attention is focused on the negative aspects of our thoughts and actions rather than the positive – and we always get what we focus on.

When Logic Won't Prevail (Monster Under The Bed)

As a child I'd lie awake at night for hours trembling with terror, knowing there was a bomb in my room and it was going to blow up any moment and kill me. I didn't have a monster under my bed because my bed was solid timber to the floor with sliding drawers inside filled with blankets. It was impossible for a monster to live there. Obviously.

Monsters, bombs, or things that go bump in the night – no matter how much the logical mind might have tried to sway us into believing otherwise, as children these terrors seemed too real to be imaginary, and yet they were. As adults, our fears are more mature in expression but just as illusory.

Fear of death and fear of lack seem to top the list for most people and although they are illusions, these fears are the foundation on which much of the world's problems are built. If we did not have a fear of death or lack there would be no reason to fight wars, to steal or lie, or inflict physical and emotional pain on others.

I was going to add fear of pain at the top of the list, but we humans seem to prefer pain over death. Our medical profession appears intent on holding patients back from death regardless of the pain they may be suffering. So, for the moment, whilst pain is something we don't want, it seems to be our society's overall preference to death, whilst suicide and euthanasia are frowned upon and in many countries, even punishable by law.

Death is an inevitable process of our Being-ness. Whether you believe in life after death or not, physical death is going to happen so why dwell on it when you can be enjoying the experience of this physical life while you're living it? Even if you don't believe in 'the afterlife', reincarnation, heaven/nirvana or any form of existence other than this physical one right now, it is still true that the thoughts we release as well as the physical things we create are all made up of our personal energy. And whilst energy can be transformed, it cannot be destroyed.

I personally believe we are eternal and infinitely creative, and the experience of 'death' is merely a return to our purest and highest form – that of soul energy. I believe that we don't ever not exist.

Lack (or loss) is the other illusion, the other 'monster under our bed'. Lack is a subjective perception. What is lack for one person is abundance for another. What constitutes lack is also subjective. Money, health and love seem to be the primary sources of our fear of lack and yet there is a limitless abundance of all these available to us because we have the ability to create them all. That is why the lack of these things is an illusion. If we don't have these things it is because we have somehow chosen for it to be that way.

I can hear you roaring furiously at me now!

"It's not my fault that I don't earn enough money from my crappy job!"

"I didn't ask to be in a car accident that has left me crippled!"

"I didn't choose to be born with a disability!"

"I wasn't the one who cheated in my marriage!"

"I've tried everything to find love but it always eludes me."

I hear you. I really do. None of us consciously chooses the uncomfortable feeling or position of lack. So, if there is a limitless abundance of everything we need and want, why don't we have it?

I suppose that some will say that there is not an abundance of everything, but I disagree. We have everything we need on this planet to feed, house and care for all of us. We have the greatest physical energy in the form of our sun to create all the power we need on the planet. And each and every one of us is born with the ability to fulfil our emotional needs and creative dreams. We are precise and highly skilled creators, so nothing is outside our abilities. Anything is possible.

I really believe that 'lack' is not an external physical phenomenon but rather, a belief we hold within ourselves. So many of us feel challenged by a lack of self-worth, education, time, social stature, family/spousal support or circumstances beyond our control, but the truth is, none of these perceived deficiencies stop us from having what we want. But the fear that they do, can.

We allow fear to hold us back from creating the most amazing and beautiful experiences in our lives and it's time we stopped! It's time to stand up to our fears. It's time to be fearless.

If you've lived in a state of fearfulness for a long time, the preceding text in this chapter may sound naïve or 'airy fairy' to you. On the other hand, you may just experience the giant lightning bolt of understanding (the "Aha!" moment) as somewhere deep inside, it all makes perfect sense. Either way, I'm going to ask you to work with me here, keep an open mind, and see where it leads you. As with everything else in this book, take what you need and leave the rest.

Releasing The Lion Within
Powerful, graceful, noble, magnificent, wise and fearless - it's no surprise that God and the Lion are often analogous in humankind's historical folklore, and religious stories. But have you ever considered that these traits are within you too?

I believe that whilst we are all physical and emotional individuals, we are also part of the spiritual, or energetic, whole. Through that energy (you might call it God, Source, Universal Soul, All That Is, etc), we are connected to all living things, and it is inherent within us, a part of us. We are made up of God Energy so it stands to reason that we also have the capacity to be powerful, graceful, noble, magnificent, wise, and yes - fearless.

For most of us, it's hard to think of ourselves as God. It feels kind of embarrassing, blasphemous and delusional to consider ourselves in the same league, even if it's true. Personally, I don't have a problem with being filled with God Energy. I've never gone around telling people I'm God because up until now I'd have probably been misunderstood (perhaps I still will be), but I believe that every single one of us is God experiencing this physical reality in order to evolve into a greater knowledge of itself. So yeah, I'm God. But so are you. Get used to it!

Whether you choose to accept yourself as God or feel more comfortable aligning yourself with the Lion, the point is to embrace the inherent power and fearlessness that is within you. That's not to say that we won't ever experience fear even when we embrace God or Lion, because fear, as our built-in early warning system, is absolutely essential in letting us know when we need to change course from a negative path to a positive one. But that's all fear is good for.

When I feel my fear starting to get out of control, I stop and take time to analyse it. I mentally work right back to the root cause (which always seems to be death or lack) and then I use the appropriate coping mechanisms to release my fear and put it in its rightful place. For example, my biggest fear is not having enough money to pay for basic needs, let alone the occasional 'want'. I've never earned a lot of money, always struggled to make ends meet and often worried about how the next bill would get paid. I'm in a lot of debt through running the Australian Songwriters Conference with no means to pay it. When the fear takes hold it can spin me into depression so fast it's crazy. Sound familiar?

Fearless Abundance

Here's what I do. I close my eyes, take some slow, deep breaths to calm myself down and then I start thinking about all the abundance I have in my life at that very moment:

- my beautiful family

- the little apartment I rent where I feel safe and at home

- a bed to sleep in tonight

- food for the next meal

- music and writing and all the creativity bursting from inside of me

- Passion for my goals and dreams

In other words, right here and right now, I'm okay. At this point I'm starting to get on top of my fear.

Appreciation leads me toward a more positive mental attitude, it draws me closer to feeling good and that's when the real magic starts. I remind myself that regardless of the fact that a bill has come in and I don't have the money to pay for it:

- there is no lack

- the Universe holds me gently and lovingly

- I'm always taken care of

- all is well

- there is truly nothing to fear.

It's at this point I let go of my fear and stop worrying about how I'm going to pay the bill. I simply ask the Universe for what I want (to have that bill paid by its due date), release it, and wait in eager anticipation for the unfolding of my request. And that's when I feel the power of God inside. I don't have to struggle because I know in my heart it will happen. I just watch in wonder because it always does. Always. It takes practice, but I know you can do this too.

The moment we think through the mind, feel through the heart and see through the eyes of God (or the Lion), we pull courage from that empowered Source within us. Fear becomes the useful 'early warning system' for which it was developed, rather than a destructive weapon that we turn upon ourselves and others.

STATEMENT 6

Anger and resentment are the two most negative and destructive emotions – learn to live without them.

Sometimes, all we need to do is

take a step back and breathe....

We have the power to
transform our thoughts
from the darkness of anger
into the lightness of joy.
There is great freedom to be found
in forgiveness,
and the deepest delight that
dwells in appreciation.

Take heart.
You have the capacity
for the noblest of all emotions...
Compassion,
empathy,
bliss.

Even in your struggle,
Remember that love is your true nature.
Allow your heart to be the sanctuary
through which to express your humanity.

Let go the pain of resentment,
and rather, feel the flood of relief
as you make room for peace
to live within your mind,
and nurture your soul.

6

If there are two emotions that eat away at us in every way, they are anger and resentment. Anger is generally recognised as being an 'in the moment' emotional response to something negative that is happening to us or around us. It is sometimes expressed in a physical way; yelling, fighting, clenched fists, gnashing teeth, vengeful thoughts etc, and sometimes people feel anger but hold it inside, unseen, simmering – you get the picture.

Resentment is an insidious creature. It can sit deep down and seethe, often in response to a hurtful situation in the past or unexpressed feelings about a negative situation. Long-held resentment flows at a deep emotional, sometimes subconscious level. I see it as the result of unmanaged or unresolved anger.

Don't get me wrong. I totally believe that it's natural to feel angry when someone does something that negatively impacts us. It's healthy, and a sign of self-love, that we choose not to accept unacceptable words or behaviour directed at us. It is completely acceptable to express our feelings in a non-violent way and tell someone how we feel about what they've done. Say it. Release it. Done.

Warning: Anger Is Bad For Your Health
Holding onto anger and resentment can have serious consequences. It is widely understood in the medical and mental health communities that anger can have a devastating

impact on our physical and psychological health. Studies have been conducted all over the world by many medical organisations and universities that indicate the health consequences of anger include heart disease, hypertension, depression, stroke, skin problems, heart attack, high blood pressure, anxiety, insomnia and even some cancers. Study the work of Lousie L. Hay, Caroline Myss and other reputable Medical Intuitives and you'll find that they believe there are many other physical consequences to holding onto anger and resentment including liver problems, chronic infections, kidney stones, weight issues, headaches and more.

Although we mainly direct our anger and resentment toward others, it would seem that the results tend to injure us more than them. There is a great analogy about resentment; it's like drinking poison in the hope it will injure someone else. That's an interesting concept, because I know that when I'm really angry at someone or resentful about something, it sits there seething below the surface making me feel stressed, depressed and sick in my stomach. I get headachy, I don't sleep well, I get really bad indigestion - and I want to eat. I'm sure the object of my distress doesn't suffer the symptoms of my angst!

Kicking The Habit
If you get angry or resentful a lot, there's good news. Chronic anger and resentment is habitual. This is a fantastic revelation because it means that, like any other habit, you can change it. You can retrain yourself and end the cycle of these negative and destructive emotions.

I spent a lot of my life feeling angry and resentful; at the school bullies who made my life hell; at my parents for their constant on again, off again relationship that caused feelings of insecurity, abandonment and mistrust; at cheating and abusive lovers whose actions attacked my self-worth; at 'The System' that never allowed me to earn enough money to do more than live hand to mouth; at people who used me and then walked away – the list is endless. No doubt as you are reading this you are working through your own list of people, situations and things that make you feel angry and resentful too.

I felt like a victim. I WAS a victim – not so much to those who had hurt me but to my own thoughts and feelings. And I was angry with myself for feeling unable to rise above the sum total of what I'd become as a result of these experiences. Can you relate to that feeling of powerlessness the way I do? The resentment seethed and riled deep within me for many years.

At around the age of 40, I began to realise that I had become an anger 'junkie'. I was permanently angry and resentful and occasionally when I wasn't, something would just seem to 'happen' to make me feel angry and resentful all over again. I had become a habitual 'user' and it had taken over my life. Once the realisation hit, I knew that I had to find a way out of it. I didn't want to feel that bad for the rest of my life. But how could I stop feeling angry and resentful toward people, situations and even myself?

A few years ago, I, along with millions of others, began to discover the Law Of Attraction. If you're not sure of what that is, there are loads of books on the topic and I recommend the book "Ask And It Is Given" by Abraham-Hicks. The basic premise of the Law Of Attraction is simple: 'what you focus on is what you get'. It makes sense. After all, the more I focused on my anger and resentment the angrier and more resentful I felt. Through the Teachings of Abraham, a group of non-physical teachers who speak through Esther Hicks, I learned that if I change the way I think, and focus on what I do want (as opposed to focusing on what I don't want), I could be happier and experience positive feelings rather than negative ones.

I wanted to feel happy, not angry, so I figured it couldn't hurt to experiment by only focusing on things that made me feel good. Have you ever tried to do that? It's really hard when you're not used to it. I'd never monitored my thoughts that closely before and I had to keep pulling myself up. I'd suddenly realise I was focusing on something that made me feel upset or angry then immediately stop and refocus my thoughts on something that made me feel good instead.

Appreciation
I began to discover something I'd had very little experience with. Appreciation. This coincided with what I was learning in Overeaters Anonymous (a 12 Step program I entered for my food addiction) where I was learning about Gratitude. I was already sending a Gratitude List to my OA sponsor each day – just five or six new things I felt grateful for; my gorgeous son, being free from my food addiction, a helpful shop assistant in the store I visited that day, etc. I learned that focusing on things I was grateful for helped me to feel better within myself.

Whilst gratitude is certainly better than any negative emotion, it didn't stop me from feeling resentful. In some ways it fuelled my resentment. Gratitude is the feeling I get when I'm indebted to someone for helping me or doing something for me. It feels a little powerless. Powerlessness and indebtedness always make me feel resentful.

Appreciation feels very different to me. It has the feeling of freedom and pure pleasure. When we are feeling appreciation about something or someone, it is virtually impossible to feel anger or resentment in that same moment. So now, I no longer feel grateful for a beautiful sunny day. I truly appreciate it. I practically roll around in that appreciation like a puppy rolls ecstatically in the warmth of a freshly turned garden bed!

Imagine living in a constant state of appreciation! Don't tell me it's impossible. I lived in a state of constant anger and resentment for so long in became a habit – and habits can be changed.

Law of Attraction and appreciation had a profound effect on my personality. I started to actively pay attention to my thoughts. This allowed me to turn them around when they became negative and instead, focus on what I really wanted to feel (joy) and what I really wanted in my life (joy!).

I stopped writing a daily Gratitude List and began writing an Appreciation List instead. The type of things I listed didn't change but the way I felt did.

I began taking time every day to appreciate. I would observe something or someone and challenge myself to find a reason to appreciate them. It became a bit of a game but now appreciation has become part of who I am. I can feel appreciation for anything! The smile of a content elderly man as he walks his dog down the street, the grace and balance of a skateboarder whizzing by, the pretty rainbow I saw after a spectacular storm, a giggling baby in the supermarket, the view of my neighbourhood from my living room window, that first cup of tea in the morning – you get the picture? As I type this, I'm appreciating my beautiful laptop that allows me the ease of writing this book for you! I can cut and paste and delete and replace words and move paragraphs around with a couple of clicks! I couldn't do that if I was using pen and paper! Massive appreciation there! ☺

I wake up in the morning to my alarm that is set to peaceful music and wriggle my toes, appreciating the warmth of my beautiful bed and the good night's sleep I've had (Lousie L. Hay taught me that one!) I appreciate everything from the breakfast I'm eating to the clothes I'm wearing to the taste of my minty toothpaste. A feeling of wellbeing and happiness pervades my being. I spend my day consciously looking for things to appreciate and I go to bed at night and appreciate the wonderful people in my life, the warmth of my comfortable bed and the good night's sleep I'm about to have.

It took time but slowly, I started to have more positive thoughts and feelings than negative ones, and my level of anger and resentment lowered dramatically. I began focusing on Now rather than the long-dead Past. I retrained myself to live in a state of appreciation and I kicked the anger and resentment habit. Now I'm an appreciation junkie! Cool!

Focusing my thoughts on appreciation certainly helped to reduce the impact of anger and resentment on my day to day life. The anger and resentment from past experiences was still there when I thought back on them, but I was choosing not to focus my energy on it. My thoughts became softer and more positive and I felt happier and healthier too.

But I wanted more than that; I wanted to find a way to dissolve the anger and resentment I felt about those past experiences completely. Was that even possible? According to this Constitutional Statement, it is.

The key lies in forgiveness. Forgiving others,
forgiving ourselves and letting go of the angst.

Forgive Thine Enemies
I know that there are many who would say that there are some actions, some deeds, that are simply unforgiveable, but I challenge that notion. There are actions and deeds that are completely unacceptable, yes. But all are forgivable. In fact, forgiving is the most loving thing we can do for our Self. When we forgive someone we are not saying "What you did is acceptable to me", we are saying "I release the impact of your actions/words from my life so I can experience peace."

Forgiveness means releasing the hurt, pain and anger,
and allowing ourselves to heal.

Sometimes people become the victims of terrible acts of cruelty and degradation. How do they survive that? How do they move forward after suffering so much? Sometimes they don't, but there are the stories of victims who not only survive, but learn to thrive and use their experience to help others. The people who find happiness again are the ones who make a decision to let go of the pain, and forgiveness seems to be at the centre of that decision.

My mother was born and raised in Holland during World War II. Her father was a member of the Dutch resistance movement and he assisted Jews to escape the country during the German Occupation. I grew up with the stories my mother had of that time, and as a young teen became fascinated with stories of the Holocaust.

If you ever need proof that the most unspeakable atrocities can be forgiven, read Eva Moses Kor's story. She and her identical twin sister, Miriam Moses, were just nine years old when they were imprisoned in the Auschwitz Concentration Camp in 1944. The rest of her family; her mother, father and two older sisters, were killed in the camp, but as identical twins, Eva and Miriam were considered the perfect 'subjects' for use in human experimentation.

There are no words to describe the horror of the torturous procedures that were forced upon Eva and Miriam and the heinous acts they witnessed inside that place, but somehow they survived, and Eva went on to become a powerful public speaker and forgiveness advocate. Now in her late seventies, Eva continues to advocate for forgiveness and the healing power it brings.

If Eva can do it, surely we can too.

There is a thought-provoking book that I read a few years ago, called 'Radical Forgiveness' by Colin Tipping. In the book, Colin suggests that the people who do wrong by us are in fact, our greatest teachers - soul mates with whom we made a contract before coming into this physical existence. He suggests that if we can learn to see them as a teacher who is, if unconsciously, fulfilling their side of the contract, we could learn to view them, and the experience they brought to us, with appreciation rather than anger. It's a really disconcerting (and Radical!) concept, but trust me, if you've been the victim of a crime or you feel victimised in any way, this book could change your life. It's a process and for some it takes time, but Radical Forgiveness has made a huge difference to the lives of thousands around the world. It certainly helped me.

Forgive Thyself – My Story
Sometimes the greatest challenge is in forgiving ourselves. Accepting our role in a situation that has caused us anger, and then forgiving ourselves for it, can be hard, especially if we've been playing the 'Blame Game' for a while.

It was incredibly hard to forgive myself for choosing to terminate a pregnancy when I was twenty-nine. I felt I had no other option and indeed, looking back at that time, I still believe I made the right choice considering the situation I was in, though I'm sure there will be those who would slam me for it. The father wanted nothing to do with it and wasn't prepared to support me or the baby, I had no money and was living hand to mouth from the government job I was employed in. Back then, the government support for single parents was negligible and there was no such thing as day care – even if I had been able to afford it. I certainly couldn't have afforded a baby sitter and if I'd stopped work to raise a baby I wouldn't have been able to pay the rent. I worked for the Department of Social Security at the time so I saw first-hand what other single mums went through. I couldn't do it. I wasn't strong enough. I was depressed and overeating again, I was frightened and I felt completely unsupported.

To say I was angry and resentful about the situation is an understatement. I'd always wanted children but that went along with the loving husband, bricks and mortar and the white picket fence ie; security. But instead I was alone, broke and an emotional mess. Feeling enraged, confused, distressed and powerless, I went into survival mode and had the pregnancy terminated.

I buried my pain for years. Even though I knew it was the right choice at the time, I never forgave myself for getting into that situation or for the choice I made. I withdrew from all intimacy, I binged on sugar and I spiralled out of control. I've only recently begun to let go of the resentment and self-hatred of myself. It's been a slow but a loving process.

Anger Management My Way
Of course, this is an extreme example, but regardless of the level of anger and resentment we might feel about any given situation, if we know how to deal with it, we can stop anger and the resulting self-abuse in its tracks. I still feel the sting of anger and resentment at times. Of course I do, but I no longer allow it to have power over my life. Here is a process I use to pull myself out of anger before it takes hold and wreaks havoc in my life:

- When a situation occurs that makes me feel angry, I step away from it and allow myself time to get over the initial anger so I can think.

- I define what is causing my anger and why.

- I think long and hard about the role I played in the situation. (Yes, MY role!)

- I look for the positive aspect of the situation that I can learn from. This is really important because there is always something to learn. It's how we expand our life experience.

- I forgive myself for getting angry and appreciate the progress I'm making. I'm now moving away from anger and resentment and toward a more positive, healthy and self-loving response.

- I decide if I need to resolve the situation that made me angry. Often, once I get to this point in the process I realise there is nothing more I need to do.

- If I feel that I do need to resolve the situation, I think about how best to utilise what I'm learning through the CUSB to help me achieve that resolution in a positive, self-empowered and loving way.

- Having done all these things, I allow myself to move forward knowing that all is well.

Appreciation and forgiveness come up in other Constitutional statements too, indicating that they play a huge role in our personal happiness and the development of our spiritual and emotional growth and potential. There is no emotion more soul-destroying than anger and resentment. It is little wonder the CUSB recommends we find a way to live without them. In walking away from anger, we give ourselves the gift of a healthier body and mind. In letting go of resentment, we give ourselves the gift of self-love and personal peace.

Great gifts indeed.

STATEMENT 7

*Be loving and kind to yourself, and you
Will find it easier to be loving and
kind to others.*

Love yourself like no one else can.

When we give of ourselves so much,
sometimes we forget to give
to the most important person...

Know you are truly worthy
of love and kindness
in your life.
Make time for You
and whatever makes you
feel special.

Take time to do things
that bring joy and appreciation
to your life,
for when you do,
you reflect that joy out to the world
and make it a better place to be.

Be gentle on yourself and
Be loving and kind to your spirit
in the same way you are
loving and kind to others,
because you deserve it so much.

When you show love to yourself
It becomes easier to give out love
and that is the most precious gift
because it is one not only given
but also received.

7

There is no one on this planet with the ability to love you the way you can, so make a commitment to love yourself every moment of your life! ☺

Many people find it really hard to be loving and kind to themselves and I admit that I'm one of them, so if you think you'll find this chapter challenging, join the club!

Most of us were raised to believe that it's egotistical, self-absorbed, arrogant or in some other way wrong to 'be in love with yourself'. And yet, it's probably the most important aspect of taking care of our well-being. Until you can learn to be loving and kind to your Self you can never truly share love and kindness with others. How can you be authentic in the giving of something so precious as love and kindness if you haven't first embraced, absorbed and nurtured it within yourself?

Self-love is the most precious gift we can give ourselves and it leads to a feeling of joy and fulfilment in our lives.

I believe that we should always put our own needs first. Before you start writing that email to me about how parents have to put the needs of their children first etc etc, please consider this: If you don't care for yourself first and foremost, who will care for your kids when you fall apart? We teach by example, so what would we be teaching our children if we drive ourselves into the ground for them or became perpetually sick, angry, depressed, frustrated and resentful?

Caring for ourselves is an obligation we should take very seriously and yet we tend to neglect it in favour of caring for everyone else instead. We put our kids, spouses, parents, friends, jobs and even our pets ahead of our own needs and suddenly that old feeling of resentment starts to creep in. It's not natural to neglect ourselves. We enter this physical life in a state of utter perfection, pure love and with a deep sense of Self. But as physical beings, we seem to forget this, so when we don't love and care for ourselves enough it causes us disharmony and dis-ease.

Stop Being Mean!
I think it starts with treating ourselves with patience and deference. I'm the first person to put myself down if I make a mistake, do something silly or can't figure something out. I apologise for myself, often laughing off my imperfections to others as though I'm inadequate or stupid and we all just have to deal with it.

A perfect example of this is my challenge with technology. I do okay on the computer considering I'm self-taught, but for years, if I haven't been able to work out how to do something I've immediately deemed myself a 'techno-moron'. I've even said this aloud to others on many occasions. Sure it sounds funny, and maybe it's a good thing that I can laugh it off, but the truth is, I'm being really mean and unfair. I'm an intelligent woman, but I can't possibly know everything, and that's okay. I would never tell someone else they were stupid or call them mean names for making a mistake or for not knowing something. How rude! Calling myself a 'techno-moron' – or any other name that deems me less than I really am - is not loving and kind, so I'm making the decision right now to stop doing it!

What about you? Do you look in the mirror and search for flaws? Do you step on the bathroom scales every single morning and then feel lousy about yourself for the rest of the day (and then do it again the next day)? Do you tell yourself you're stupid every time you don't know the answer to something? Do you look at people around you and wish you were just half as beautiful, smart, thin, stylish, articulate, confident, (insert your adjective here) as they are?

Will you join me in the decision right here, right now, to stop calling yourself names, chiding and belittling yourself and putting yourself down? It won't be easy for us, you know. It's a habit that will take time to break, but I think that if we concentrate on being more aware of our self-talk, we can nip this problem in the bud really quickly.

Developing a loving and positive vocabulary for our self-talk is important. Next time you think or say a 'put down' to yourself – STOP! Instead, try saying something like *"I'm really proud of myself for giving this a go"* or *"At least I'm trying and with practice I might even get better at this"* or *"I made a mistake but I'll try to do better next time"*. And how about this beauty:

> *"I am a valuable and beautiful gift to this planet and I appreciate me just the way I am."*

Write them down and keep them in your pocket or purse so you can pull them out and use them anytime the negative self-talk starts to kick in.

The Temple
Taking care of our body is one of the most loving and kind things we can do for ourselves. This physical aspect of our being-ness is the temple for our soul while we are here on this planet. We rely on it to function well for us and to provide amazing sensory experiences, but we need to keep it healthy and treat it with the reverence it deserves.

A healthy diet and regular exercise play a huge role of course, and most of us do our best to ensure that we eat well, get the rest we need and do some form of physical activity. Every body (literally) is different, so using our intuition and gut instincts about food and exercise is a good way to go. Being healthy does not mean you have to be a size 8! I believe that being healthy means nourishing your body and maintaining it in such a way that you feel comfortable in your daily activities and exertions.

For those of you with an addiction like me, I know how hard it can be to maintain a healthy body. All addictions affect our physical, emotional and spiritual health, so we must take extra care and show ourselves even more love and respect, if our bodies and minds are to function long and well.

Writing this chapter has been difficult. As I was beginning it I was also in the process of acknowledging to myself that I had started over-eating again, after nearly five years of abstaining. It was a devastating admission that rocked me to my core. How could I write about being loving and kind to the Self when I was doing something that was so self-destructive, unloving and distressing to myself?

Once I realised what was happening I knew I had to make a choice. I could continue on the path I was on (overeating and binging) which would lead me to certain early death, or find new ways to deal with life's challenges. I realised that I needed to adopt new coping mechanisms.

For several years I had relied on the love and support of a very dear friend and soul mate to help get me through challenging times without overeating. But I lost my friend in early 2012, and with no knowledge of how to emotionally support myself, I had returned to this old means of coping.

Writing the book has certainly helped me. In examining the CUSB so closely and frequently, I've found it's becoming an established and ingrained part of my daily life. I guess it's a natural process. When we live with something constantly, it must at some point become a part of who we are.

Here are healthy, loving ways I cope with challenges instead of falling prey to my addiction:

- I rest as much as I can. I go to bed earlier and take short 'time-outs' through the day to close my eyes, breathe deeply and gently, and rebalance my Self.

- I connect with positive, supportive people I trust and talk to them about what is happening with me. Honesty with myself and those around me is such an important aspect of addiction recovery.

- I work from home a lot, but I stay connected with family, friends and clients as much as I can so I don't get depressed or start to 'hibernate'.

- I take advantage of Social Networking by connecting with friends and followers on Facebook, Twitter and Skype. It's entertaining and I feel good sharing with people.

- I write in my online Journal regularly and this helps me a lot. Being accountable to my readers is incredibly important to me. I don't want to let them or myself down.

- I read inspirational work - including the CUSB statements! - and I implement all the beautiful and loving advice of my favourite Mind-Body-Spirit authors and teachers.

- I go for a walk. This helps to clear my head and I know it's healthy for my body which makes me feel good.

- Each day I pre-plan my meals for the next day and I stick to it.

I've been reading, writing and teaching inspirational, motivational, affirmative and life-changing work for years. Writing this chapter (and in fact this entire book) gives me more than an opportunity to share my thoughts with you. It is reminding me of all the ways I can cope with life's challenges in a healthy and positive way - willingly, consciously and conscientiously LIVING it for myself!

'Me' Time
The birth of the Industrial Revolution brought with it the promise of incredible inventions and time-saving devices all designed to make life easier and more comfortable. This was especially true for women who, until the fifties, spent most of their lives doing long, hard hours of housework.

I remember when I was very young, five or six years old, watching my mother toil away at her big old barrel of a washing machine with its twin rollers to squeeze the water out using a handle that she turned manually with effort. When my mother was a child in Holland, her mother had used a boiler over a wood burning stove and a special paddle to hand wash and beat the dirty laundry. Nowadays, we have fully automatic washing machines that do everything without us having to be there at all; truly a time and labour saving device.

Running hot water, electricity, white goods, power tools, computers; newer, faster, better, smarter, smaller, efficient, time saving devices – all designed to get the work done quickly and give people more time and freedom do the things they really wanted to do.

So why is it that today, people still have so little time for themselves?

It seems that rather than using their newfound free time to relax and enjoy their lives, people have just filled up that time with more 'stuff' and business (busy-ness). Some people feel guilty if they are not doing something and some think they want or need more 'stuff'. Some just don't know what to do with free time. Either way, they feel compelled to work longer and harder to be busy doing things for others or earning the money to buy more of the said 'stuff'. It's a vicious and self-defeating cycle of time consumption - a bit like my Grandmother's hand washing. All that toil and bother then and now.

I used to be constantly filling my time to the point of physical and emotional exhaustion. I didn't know myself at all and I rarely took time out to nurture my Being. There was too much to do, family commitments, work, friends – constantly doing, rarely being. These days I schedule time off – 'Me Time' - in my diary. I don't use it to write or help someone out or do the laundry or anything else that isn't a 100% completely self-nurturing activity or experience.

I rest, I read or watch inspiring, romantic or funny books and movies. I walk along the beautiful waterfront near my home or on one of our stunning local beaches, or I wander around our local New Age and Alternative Health locale just to absorb the feeling of light, love and joy I feel there. I'm so appreciative of the beauty of the area I live in and I take advantage of it every chance I get.

'Me' time is time on my own to refresh my mind, connect with my spirit and rest my body. Please do this for yourself as much as you can. It is so important. I know it's hard to find time, especially when you have kids, but you CAN do it! I have 'Me Time' when Mason is at school or when he is with his father, or I organise for him to spend a Saturday or have a 'sleepover' with my mother. Mason's adores his "Oma"!

If you are not taking 'Me Time' for yourself it's because you are not choosing to do so, not because you don't have time. So, clear some time regularly for yourself and not only will you feel better, you'll be much more fun to be around!

Obligation

Ugh! I loathe the word! For me, the implication is of being made to do something even though I don't want to. The way I see it, if I feel obligated to do anything, I'm doing it for the wrong reason. It's not in my best interest, or my higher nature, to do things I don't want to do.

I believe that we only have one obligation: to be and do that which brings joy into our own lives.

Someone recently disagreed with me about this, suggesting that we all have obligations to meet such as caring for and raising our children, doing what our boss asks of us, paying our bills etc. I understand the direction from which this response comes but my feeling is that I care for and raise my child from a place of love, not obligation. I pay my bills with joy because I appreciate the goods and services with which I've been provided, and if I work for someone else it's because I enjoy the job and the tasks that are set for me. If whatever I'm doing does not bring me joy or come from a place of love, then I have a serious look at why, and make some changes that suit me better. Sometimes it's simply my thoughts that need changing and sometimes the change requires physical action.

If I'm doing something out of obligation rather than because I love it and want to do it, then I'm letting myself down. It's not someone else's job to make me happy or give me what I want. It's MY job. It's not my job to make you happy or give you what you want – it's YOUR job. Sure, I'll support and inspire you along the way, but I'll do that because I want to, because I love supporting and inspiring others. I do it because it's a joyful thing for me to do.

That may sound selfish but it's not. You see, I believe that when I do something for you because I want to and it brings me joy, then I'm sending my positive energy into the Universe/All That Is/Eternity which effects everything and everyone around me in a positive way – including you. So even though I'm doing it for me, I'm automatically doing it for all. When I do anything because I feel obligated, I'm sending out a negative energy that will negatively impact all around me. Would you rather receive my positive energy or my negative energy?

Do Unto Others
…as you would have others do unto you? Maybe. I prefer 'Do unto others as you would do unto yourself.' It puts the responsibility right back where it belongs. I believe we are all connected and I have observed that the way we treat our Self is often reflected in the way we treat others. If we consistently treat ourselves with love and kindness it stands to reason that we will be more likely to treat others in the same way. Why? Because when we feel good, when we appreciate who we are and show loving kindness toward ourselves we naturally give out those feelings. It's the energy we put out to the world and we can't possibly treat others in a negative way. As with obligation, if we consistently neglect our Self in favour of others we will at some point reflect our feelings of frustration, anger, stress and blame onto those around us.

So, be fair to yourself and the people in your life. Put yourself first, and show some loving kindness toward the beautiful, perfectly imperfect and special person that is You. Not only will you be honouring yourself, you'll be reflecting your bright light of love and kindness out into the world.

STATEMENT 8

The love, respect and friendship of others is a privilege, not a right.

When we bond with someone
in a loving and respectful way
we can experience the boundless
beauty, wisdom and truth that is

Relationship in Harmony...

There is no greater gift
we can give ourselves and others
than the commitment of
authentic love and friendship.

We are intimately connected
through Spirit and God-love,
and we are linked by limitless
threads of appreciation and joy.

As we share our deepest and most
divine aspects with others,
we begin to understand the power of
true friendship, love and respect.

So be intent on giving honestly
and wholeheartedly of yourself,
and it will be returned to you
a thousand-fold.

8

Deceptive in its simplicity, this Statement of the Constitution seems obvious, but for me, it presents something of a dichotomy. In accordance with our most dominant State of Being - our spiritual, Soul State - we are already surrounded by, and part of, the intrinsic love, reverence and relationship that is the Universal God Force. In essence, it is what we are and we can never be separated from it.

As non-physical beings having a physical experience (I love Abraham's definition for us), or as many would say, as children of God, we are always loved. We can always rely on God-Love and Self-Love, which to my mind is the same thing because I believe we are all part of Universal God Force. God-Love/Self-Love always exists, whether we are consciously aware of it or not.

We can even rely on Collective Soul-Love, ie; the compassion each of our souls has for all other souls regardless of time, space and the differences in our physical experience. Giving our time and money to charities and disaster relief efforts is a good example of Collective Soul-Love. No matter what we do, the Collective Soul cannot not love itself.

What we can't rely on, is that in our physical, Human State of Being, those around us in their physical, Human State of Being will automatically love us too. The dichotomy exists because we are born with the intrinsic belief that it is a right (which it is) but in our Human existence, life's not like that. So, it is a right - and yet it isn't.

Of course, in this world, we all understand that we need to form human relationships in order to also form love, respect and friendship. Our human existence compels us to connect with others for all our experiences. But what happens if family members don't like each other, or when we have a relationship with someone who appears to not understand this premise? What happens if cultural, religious or political beliefs differ?

Respect for all living things, and for each other's physical and personal rights, opinions and boundaries, is something we can all practice. We are never going to agree with everyone about everything and that's fine. But no one's opinion is 'wrong', because opinions are subjective. So are beliefs, rights and boundaries.

Try to conceive of a respect-filled world where right and wrong don't exist. Think about it. There would be no need for debate, argument or one-upmanship. There would be nothing to prove. There would be no need for wars to defend the righteous or to defeat the infidels or uphold our beliefs. If we could respect everyone's right to believe what they want, and respect the boundaries of others, even if those beliefs and boundaries are different to our own –WOW! I wonder if we, in our Human State of Being, will ever evolve to that point on a global level. It would certainly bring us into much closer alignment with our spiritual State of Being.

John Lennon beseeched us to visualise a world like this in his beautiful song, 'Imagine'. The question is; how do we even begin to achieve that? Is it even possible? I choose to believe it is. We can choose to see the people around us as the perfect Soul Beings they are and make the decision to treat them with the love and respect they deserve. It's been done before. Our world has seen individuals who have achieved this extraordinary level of unconditional love and respect for others: Jesus Christ, Mother Teresa, The Dalai Lama, Ghandi – and countless others who go about their lives lovingly, respectfully and unconditionally giving service to others. They are a hard act to follow, but worthy of our effort, don't you think?

In the meantime, what can we do to draw love, respect and friendship into our lives? And how can we draw people to us with whom we can confidently share this privilege?

Birds of a Feather
Growing up, I was always taught to be respectful and kind toward others and 'to do unto others as you would have others do unto you.' My Grandmother used to quote this to me when I was young and I guess I had an expectation that if I was nice to people they would be nice to me. It didn't take long for this theory to be disproved as I spent most of my childhood and teenage years trying to be nice to people who beat and bullied me anyway. So, obviously, showing love, respect and friendship toward others does not necessarily mean they will reciprocate. Or does it?

I think the answer partly lies in how we treat ourselves. In the last chapter we discussed how loving ourselves makes it easier to love others. I think the way we treat our Self gives others a guide as to how they can treat us too. We draw forth from others the exact expectations we have of our Selves. If we display self-respect, we will draw respectful people to us. If we are filled with self-criticism we will draw critical people to us. If we don't like our Self much, we will draw people who won't like us (or themselves) much either. I didn't feel any self-worth growing up, so I attracted people who would demonstrate that worthlessness to me. Birds of a feather...

This is the Law of Attraction at work. It plays such a huge role in our lives so it's good to know that we have absolute power over it – whether we know it or not. We can consciously choose to treat ourselves in a loving, respectful and friendly way and by doing so, draw people with the same qualities into our life. When we treat ourselves and others well, the Universe reflects that back to us again and again and our desire for caring relationships is fulfilled. Not only that, if people do occasionally pass through our lives who don't appear to reflect how we feel about ourselves or who don't treat us in a kind and respectful way, we know that either we are not giving out kindness and respect, or we are not being kind and respectful to our Self.

Another aspect of this scenario is how we manage our reaction to someone who treats us in a less than deserving way. I have found that even when someone treats me badly or disrespectfully, it doesn't hurt as much because my focus is not on how they treat me but on how I treat me. If I am genuinely happy with who I am, if I'm showing myself love and respect and I like myself, then it's not my problem if someone else feels differently. I still try to show that person some compassion (though it's not always easy!) because I figure maybe they don't have a lot of love, respect and friendship in their life.

Love Is A Many Splendid Thing
They say it makes the world go 'round, yet love seems to be one of the most volatile and dynamic of all our emotions. Throughout history, humans have lived for it, died for it, broken rules, hearts and sanity over it - even killed for it. Love seems to have a spectacularly unpredictable effect on us and yet we all crave it in our lives. Of course, love is a beautiful thing. It makes us feel valuable and cared for. It makes us feel alive. Love exists for us on a number of levels and we've covered a few of them in earlier chapters; love of Self, Universal/God love, compassion, etc.

The most 'human' aspect of love is Romance with a capital R, because it's tied to the primitive and instinctual physical acts of sex and procreation, as well as emotional attachment. On the surface, this is the love we seem to desire the most and whether we have it, don't have it, had it and lost it, give it to someone who doesn't give it back, or get it from someone we don't want it from – whatever; its effect on us is powerful.

More songs, poems and books have been (and continue to be) written about love than any other subject. We are obsessed with it.

Romantic relationships are profoundly affected by the level of love, respect and friendship underlying them. We don't necessarily need to be friends with a person in order to show them compassion, and we can respect a person without feeling affection for them. We can even know a person well without feeling love or respect for them. But for a romantic (or any other meaningful personal relationship) to survive and thrive there has to be a deep and equal exchange of love, respect and friendship at its core.

R.E.S.P.E.C.T.
Tell you what it means to me. It means being aware and considerate of the differences in people around us and understanding that we are all equal, special and perfect in our imperfection. Whether we are talking about basic human rights, the right to make personal choices, the right to personal beliefs, or the right to exist, respecting others and ourselves is the key to our peaceful and joyful co-habitation of this planet.

Being respectful and having respect shown toward us is a two-way street. I spend a lot of time at my son's primary school and occasionally I'll hear the old line about "kids not having any respect these days". But respect is something one has to experience in order to understand and reciprocate. I've noticed that children show the same level of respect that they are given. I think it's true for adults as well. But there are two types of respect and they each compel a different response.

Fear-based respect is the one offered to people who are in a position of power and who choose to misuse it or wield it like a sword over the heads of their subordinates. We've all known people like this. More often than not, the 'respect' these people receive from others is fabricated, surface-deep and easily lost. Fear-based respect leads to discord, defection and outright mutiny. People who lead with fear-based respect don't get a lot of dinner invitations.

People who interact with fairness, compassion, strength and appreciation command love-based respect. These are the people who are highly regarded, even adored, by everyone around them. They lead by example and try to make others feel at ease. Rather than use and abuse others, they value people and encourage the best from them through positive reinforcement and acknowledgment. In return, they receive a high level of loyalty, affection and admiration.

You've Got To Have Friends
Friendship is based on connection and trust. It can't exist without them. Getting to know someone, finding common ground and developing confidence in them, takes time. Sometimes it takes no time at all when Soul Mates come together in friendship. They recognise each other almost instantly and the bond is deep, immediate, and it tends to affect their lives forever.

Friendships create a platform for many of our most meaningful life experiences. Our friends are often a reflection of ourselves, though they may have a variety of backgrounds, personalities, careers, beliefs, lifestyles and financial circumstances. There is always a commonality to be found and it's usually in one of these life aspects, however it's the differences between friends that allows them to explore and experience their individual and collective growth and evolution.

One of the things I'm beginning to understand is that the health of our friendships is a litmus test for the health of our minds. True friends will always be honest with each other because they care. That takes a lot of trust because the more we care about someone the less we want to hurt their feelings or worse, lose them from our lives.

Being honest with a friend means not only do we have to trust they will know we love and care for them enough to be honest, we also have to trust in our ability to weather their anger, hurt or even their complete withdrawal from us if our honesty is not acceptable to them. The reverse is also true. The best friends to have are the ones who don't let us get away with acting, reacting or otherwise being, 'less than' they know we really are. A true friend will tell us if they think we are being a dick, a dork or a diva. They are our cheer squad and our firing squad all wrapped up in one, and we just have to love them for it.

It is a great privilege to have the love respect and friendship of others – much more satisfying than if it were simply a right or expectation. When our relationships reflect these three things, we know we are evolving and expanding in a positive and loving way. Though conflicts in our personal, communal and global human relationships occur, it allows us the opportunity to rise above our primal fears and seek out resolution in loving, respectful and cordial ways. It's up to us to make it happen and I believe we can.

As with everything else, it takes just one mindful thought, a conscious choice from you and me to create what we want in our lives. If each one of us would consciously choose to live in loving, respectful and friendly relationship with every other person on this planet, then just like the Butterfly Effect, we could watch with wonder as true peace and harmony ripples throughout humanity and changes the world.

Imagine that.

STATEMENT 9

You can make changes in yourself, but you cannot force changes in others.

The Power Of Change Is Yours

You can be whatever you choose to be.
You have the power to change
the way you view the world,,
to alter your perception of life,
and become the person
you most want to be because

...you are here to learn and grow.

There is nothing to stop you
from reaching for the highest,
most beautiful and joyful
version of You.
It is your birth right
and your soul's desire

... to live a life of delightful increase.

As you transform yourself,
You will sense the flow of energy
that radiates through you.
Feel the powerful shift within
as you draw from the absolute
perfection of your Being

...and continue to evolve with love.

9

If you have a compulsive disorder, an addiction, or you frequently find yourself trying to resolve the personal problems of others, you might be challenged by this Statement. I know that I was.

Change is a natural part of life. It's inescapable, which is a good thing, because without it we would have no reason to be here. Change causes us to grow and evolve; it should be embraced as a joyful experience. Why then, do we feel so challenged by it?

Perhaps it's because we tend to look upon a change as being either positive or negative in nature when in fact, change is just change. Neither good nor bad, change is movement only. It's in our personal perception to change, that the positive or negative aspects are created – how we view and react to change is a choice.

What if we were able to experience an unexpected change and instead of saying "Oh no, this is awful!" we said "Well, this is different!" Can't you just feel the difference in the vibration, the energy, of these two statements?

Why is it sometimes hard to make changes in our own life, all the while trying to force our opinions and choices on to others in the hope that they will see our point of view and change? Maybe we need to clean up our own house and let the neighbours take care of themselves!

Becoming a Certified Professional Coach was life changing for me because one of the first things I learned in the training sessions is that a good coach doesn't have the right answers (Shock! Horror!) A good coach asks the right questions.

I love that notion because it's a reminder that each one of us already has access to the solution for every problem. I believe we are born with the knowledge of the Universe within us, that it's a natural part of the evolutionary process, and we not only carry the physical evolvement of our ancestors forward through generations, but also the evolvement of mind, thought and spiritual understanding.

In being Human, we sometimes do need help to figure it all out, but the answers are all there within, just waiting to be rediscovered. As a life coach, I know it's not my job to tell my clients what to do. It IS my job to help them uncover all the options they have so they can choose for themselves what solutions will work best for them.

When I was in a 12 Step program for my food addiction, I had a 'sponsor' and I also sponsored others. As sponsors we were taught never to give advice or tell our 'sponsees' what to do. Rather, we were encouraged to share our personal experiences of dealing with our addiction and other issues. The sponsee could perhaps take something of our experience and utilise it in their life if it felt right to them.

Writing this book is a great example. I'm sharing my experiences and sharing the variety of options I have uncovered and the emotional healing processes and practices I've developed. I want this book to inspire, motivate and give hope to you, my reader, but I won't try to force you to think the way I think or do things my way. I am simply sharing what I've discovered, my understanding of the CUSB, everything I've learned in my life, and how it all corresponds for me. This is how life works for me, and if there is anything within these pages that rings true for you, I invite you to utilise it to see if it works in your life. Or not. The choice is always yours.

That leads us to the core of this Statement. There are an infinite number of choice variations for every situation, every challenge. The choices for change I make are based on my life experience and understanding of what feels right for me. As individuals with varying life experiences, we can only ever make changes that are in harmony with our Self, to cause our own personal growth and balanced State of Being. And that's the way it's supposed to be, from an evolutionary perspective, for how could we evolve as Beings without the input of new and differing ideas, choices, changes and variations in thought?

Life is full of change. We wouldn't have life - and perhaps there would be no reason for this physical world to exist at all - without change. We love to experience new things. We love to create and to cause changes in our life and in our world. It's what we live for. If we all thought the same things, made the same choices or followed one central idea, there would be no growth, no expansion - no evolution.

So why do we constantly try to change others if in doing so threatens the continued evolution of our individual and collective States of Being?

A Change for the Better
When we try to force someone to do what we want, both parties automatically place a lot of negative energy into the situation. The outcome won't be what we want at all, and even if it seems to be, there won't be any lasting satisfaction or joy in it. We might feel irritation or frustration as we struggle to control the other person to do our will, and they might feel anger, fear or powerlessness as they are forced to do something they don't want to do. With all that negative energy swirling around, the results cannot possibly be fruitful.

In my life, I've discovered that change works the same way. Forcing change is like struggling against the tide. These days, when a change is needed in any area of my life, I think about all the opportunities that are available so I can seek out the one that feels right. I look to my feelings and intuition, as they are the best indicators of what I want (or don't want) for myself.

My process is simple. I think about an option to see if it feels good. Does it give me a feeling of relief, enthusiasm, joy and empowerment, or do I feel pessimistic, discouraged, unenthusiastic and powerless? Does the supporting feeling of that option come from a place of love or fear? Does the choice make me want to fly or does it give me that sinking feeling?

We've all made changes or choices that make us feel bad because we think it will be best for everyone concerned or better for us 'in the long run'. But how often do those changes and choices really work out well for us? How happy do they really make us feel in the long term?

Listen To Me!
We each experience life from our own individual point of view, based on our reactions to change, knowledge and observation of the world around us.

Learning from the experience of others can be beneficial to us too, but only if we willingly invite it in. No one likes to have someone else's ideology forced upon them. We all know someone who just loves to help by going out of their way to offer their veritable ocean of great advice. These people are always right and any disagreement with, or deviation from, their plan of action to sort out your life is met with immediate rebuke.

I call it the 'Listen To Me' Syndrome (LTMS) and it's a condition that affects us all from time to time, though some unfortunate individuals seem permanently afflicted. I don't see the point in giving unasked-for advice because it is almost always viewed by the recipient as intrusive and will often fall on deaf ears anyway. Forcing our opinions and advice onto others can cause them to feel powerless, stressed and angry. None of these emotions will help them to make positive changes in their life. I avoid people with LTMS like they have the Plague!

I've learned that I am more helpful to people if I close my mouth and open my ears. Listening is the most loving thing I can do for someone who is going through changes or wanting to make changes in their life. I believe we all have the knowledge of the Universe inside us, therefore we are capable of finding our own answers. So what right do I have to impose my advice on anyone?

We all have the capacity to work through our own 'stuff' but sometimes people do want help to sort through their issues. As a professional coach, I've learned to ask the right questions to prompt my clients to think through to the answer themselves. That's an empowering exercise. My favourite questions are "What is the problem?", "How do you feel about that?", "Why do you feel that way?" and "What are the options or solutions you can see to resolve this issue?" Often, my client will come up with the answer with very little prompting. Ask the right questions and they almost always find the answers that feel right for them.

Have you ever noticed that you can sit and mull a problem over in your head and nothing seems to makes sense, but when someone is willing to just sit and listen, it can make a huge difference? I think it's the physical action of speaking out loud that is the key. Perhaps it is a left-brain/right-brain mechanism. When we use the physical function of speaking, maybe it sparks the practical, logical, clear-sightedness of the left-brain into action, or perhaps it allows space in our creative right-brain to open up to inspired ideas, or possibly, it balances out of our left- and right-brain functions to allow us to figure things out better. Whatever it is, allowing someone to 'talk it out' while we listen really does seem to work.

By developing great listening skills we can be truly helpful to others when they need us. The answers they come up with and the choices they make may be very different to the ones we would choose, but that's okay too. We each have to do what is right for ourselves and our personal situation. That's how we all evolve and expand.

That's how change occurs.

We can discover interesting options that are out there for us, and make choices based on the experiences of others. That's not to say that our own perception is flawed, but sometimes we are bound by the limitations of our own experience. Not everything that works for me will also work for you, and vice versa, but sometimes it's fun to try new and different things, just to find out!

Adapting to Change
Adapting to change with finesse is a learned skill. In the past, change always evoked a high level of stress and anxiety for me, but I've learned that fear of change is like fear of the unknown. It really is an unsubstantiated reaction borne of feeling insecure and defenceless. The thing is, when we understand that change cannot ever truly harm us, it becomes much easier to accept and even embrace it.

I have a list of affirming thoughts for dealing with changes in my life and they help me enormously:

- I cannot ever truly die. My Soul-Self, the greatest, most authentic aspect of me, is eternal.

- Change is only change - it is neither good nor bad. It just is.

- I can choose how I react to change in my life. I choose to focus on the positives.

- Change brings new opportunities that allow me to grow and expand.

- There are no accidents. There are no coincidences. Everything happens for a reason.

- I relax in the knowledge that all is well in my life. I go with the flow.

- Remaining calm in the midst of great change is an empowering exercise.

These affirming thoughts allow me the freedom to try new experiences on for size without fear. Changing our thoughts to access positive and joyful experiences is a simple process. That doesn't mean it's an easy one or that it automatically works the first time we try. It has taken me a long time to feel like I'm starting to get it right.

My Story
One of the most profound experiences that led me to change my thoughts and focus occurred in 2007. I was spending time with a friend, and we were talking about health issues. I felt really comfortable with this friend even though we'd only known each other for a few months, so I confided my health fears to him. I was seriously overweight at 140kg (308lbs) and I was terrified that I was headed for a heart attack or stroke. My biggest fear was in leaving my then four year-old son without a mother, and I was devastated beyond words that, no matter how hard I tried, what diet I went on, or exercise regime I laboured through, nothing seemed to work. In fact, even though I'd lose some weight, in the end I couldn't maintain it and would always put the weight back on – and then some. As a result, I felt exhausted, depressed, in physical pain and completely defeated.

My friend turned to me and said that he understood how I felt. I almost laughed out loud because he was slim, strong and healthy, with glowing skin and energy to burn. This person couldn't possibly have any idea how I felt. But I was wrong. He told me of his own battle with food and how it had affected him. He told me he was a compulsive overeater and showed me photos of him when he was younger and much bigger. He explained about the 12 Step program, Overeaters Anonymous, that he lives by and asked if I'd like to go to the next meeting with him to check it out and see if it felt right for me. I said yes.

My friend saved my life that day, though he continues to deny it. It's true that I made the choice to be willing to try this new experience. I accepted the change into my life and through the program I changed the way I thought about food, my eating, my emotions and my relationships. For the first time, I even recognised my faults and weaknesses and that was tough. Never before, had I consciously accepted my role in the mess that was my life. Big changes indeed.

At times it was a painful process, and I didn't do the program perfectly. I still struggle with aspects of it. But that day in 2007, my life changed, and it changed for the better because I accepted the gift of experience that my friend shared with me. With a ready heart and an open mind I willingly made a change. I chose to let go of the past hurts, pain and guilt, and in the process, I let go of a lot of the weight that I'd been holding onto since childhood. I still carry some weight around with me, testament that I've not yet completely overcome the issues that I'm addressing, but then, as I recall, I'm perfectly imperfect and that's okay.

I believe we draw all experiences into our life. I also believe that we can alter habits, attract people and things, and change the world with the thoughts we choose to focus on. This belief has given me the power of responsibility over how I deal with change, the choices I make – and the experiences I have as a result. Now THAT's true empowerment! We are moving back into the realm of Law of Attraction here; we get what we focus on, our thoughts become our reality, and so on.

Making or dealing with changes in our life with grace, acceptance, fearlessness and a positive attitude, turns fear and doubt of a future out of our control, into a fun and joyful game, as we pick and choose our direction with confidence and absolute certainty. I admit that I haven't completely mastered it yet, but I'm having so much fun trying, and when it works - Oh! The joy, connectedness and self-empowerment feels so good!

STATEMENT 10

You can lead, but you cannot force others to follow.

Leadership Wisdom

Everyone has their own path.
No two people hold
the exact same dream
in their heart so
help others reach their goals
as you reach for yours.
Be a leader worth following.

When others seek your guidance,
be joyful and enthused.
Sharing the best of who you are
will encourage the best from others,
so walk your path with integrity,
humility and strength.
Be earnest in your leadership.

Be the leader of your own life,
be your own guide and
your own master,
and remember that
the guiding of others
is an art and a privilege.
Be honourable in your task.

10

The best definition I've ever heard for good leadership came from Neale Donald Walsch (best-selling author of the 'Conversations With God' book series) at a recent seminar. He said, "A true leader doesn't say "Follow me". A true leader says, "I'll go first".

Whether it's at home, in the workplace, at school, in politics, or the local gym, leadership means more than setting a good example. It means being a good example - of humility, honour, fairness and compassion, so that others may choose to be the same. Or not. The choice is theirs and it's a valid one.

We can all be leaders. We each have the capacity to teach and guide others. We have experiences and knowledge to share, and there are always people seeking to learn and grow as they travel their life's path. But perhaps, most important of all, we can behave like leaders, regardless of whether others choose to follow or not.

To me, a leader is someone who understands the 'goals' that need to be achieved and has a plan to reach them. The plan includes working effectively with others, utilising their talents, and guiding and assisting them to reach the goals too. Leadership also suggests a necessary proficiency, knowledge-base or skill-set in order to achieve the tasks at hand.

Leaders & Dictators

Just because something works for me, doesn't mean it applies to everyone. I was such a 'bossy boots' as a kid. I believed I always knew best and I always had to be right. I rarely listened properly to the thoughts and opinions of others. I was too busy formulating my intelligent, opposing or humorous response. I thought I had brilliant leadership qualities because I believed I knew best and was good at telling others what to do. Hmmm...

Forcing others to do our will doesn't make us leaders, nor does it make them 'followers'. It makes us bullies and them, resentful victims. A bully will never be a true leader because leadership required respect – on both sides. Forcing others to believe what we believe, think as we think or do what we want them to do is not leadership, its dictatorship. It's also contrary to the evolvement of our Being.

A Leader is the one who goes first, who paves the way, inspires others to greatness and shares the victory spoils. A dictator sits behind the front-line troops, tells others what to do, demands subservience and takes full credit for the victories.

Great leaders don't develop great followers, they develop more great leaders; they are not focused on being 'in charge', but rather, they are eager to seek out the strengths and skills of others and give them opportunities to lead too. Great leaders display humility, responsibility and integrity.

It can be incredibly challenging to deal with a Dictator in our life –especially if they are in a position to cause us pain or discomfort. If you have a boss who is your own personal nightmare, you know exactly what I'm talking about. So, how do you deal with that?

My Story

Forcing others to follow our lead at the expense of their well-being is counterproductive. I've certainly learned that the hard way – and from opposite sides of the table...

I remember the worst boss I ever had. He was the owner and manager of the business - a tall, bulky, mean-tempered man, who literally stood over his staff and screamed at them – even in front of customers. His face would go purple with rage and he'd bellow at the top of his lungs as he stood over some poor soul who'd be cowering at their desk wondering if they'd escape alive at 5pm. I'd watch with fascination and horror when he did this, wondering if he'd give himself an aneurism. I vowed I would never allow him to bully me like that.

The day came, of course. I can't remember my transgression. I sat at my Reception desk and the Dictator went at it. He bent over me, screamed into my face, started going purple – the whole performance. I sat there, determined to keep my face neutral as I rehearsed the lines I'd practiced in my head, and when he was forced to take a breath between screeching, I put my hand up between us and very firmly (!!) said, "STOP!"

He looked a little startled that I'd dared to speak in the middle of his tirade. I'd called his bluff so I kept going. "Don't you EVER speak to me that way again! If you're not happy with something I've done, tell me so I can change it but don't you EVER yell at me or treat me this way again because I don't deserve it and I won't put up with it!!" I pushed up out of my chair, forcing him to step back, and walked over to the coffee machine. I was shaking like hell but so proud of myself that I didn't care if he fired me. He didn't, and you know what? He never yelled at me again either. Actually he was quite nice to me after that, though other staff didn't escape his wrath. It was an awful environment to work in and I left a few months later. I truly appreciate that experience now and consider my Dictator to be a blessing, because he made me stand up for myself, and also taught me the value of true leadership simply by his lacking in that department.

Conversely, the greatest leaders and influences in my life have been those closest to me. One such Leader was a dear friend and confidante who loved and supported me through many stresses and life challenges – and I lost him because I constantly tried to force my agenda. In a compulsive, driven and fearful state, I became an emotional vampire, sucking the life out of the friendship in an effort to stay afloat. I relied on him for all my emotional nourishment instead of seeking it within myself, and eventually my compulsive and emotional State drove him away.

Though we've never spoken of it, I know he walked away, not only to protect his own State of emotional wellbeing, but also to allow me the opportunity to find the strength to stand on my own two feet. In his own way, though I know it broke both our hearts, he showed immense leadership, just as he always has, in guiding me to a place I needed (and unconsciously wanted) to be; a place where I now confidently and competently support my physical, emotional and spiritual Self. Though totally devastated by his leaving, I feel eternal gratitude for the legacy he left behind.

Leading with compassion and strength is a learned ability, I think. It takes humility and patience, and there is a certain level of self-control involved. But there must also come a time of letting go, of leading someone to a point where they can fly on wings of their own. That's what my friend did, and I now realise it was one of his most loving acts toward me.

Trail-Blazing
We all have our individual paths to follow. Sometimes we are joined on our journey by others who may be on the same or similar path, and sometimes we walk alone. If we choose to follow someone else's lead, we do so because we trust the leader's wisdom and ability and we believe that, ultimately, it will be of benefit to us. If others choose to follow our lead, the

same deal applies, and it's up to us to be honourable in our leadership, blazing a trail that is worthy of them.

Using the CUSB as a guide, I am developing greater confidence and strength as I follow my own path through life. I'm learning to trust myself, my intuition and instincts, and I have very little fear of the future. Past pains are no longer the burden on my psyche they used to be, and I live with joy as the predominant emotion now, rather than the deep depression and sadness I once knew. I used to have self-trust issues around my ability to lead myself (let alone others), but these days, I feel comfortable following a path of my choosing and helping others to do the same.

You can do this too. Regardless of where you are now in your life, you can take courage from those who have gone before you and the knowledge and strength they have imparted, and blaze your own trail. Blaze a trail so big and beautiful that you make it easy for others to follow in your footsteps if they choose.

I think that's the real point; being a leader doesn't mean you must have others to lead, after all, isn't it more important to your Being that you lead your own life and let others do as they will? If you've 'got it all together' people will tend to gravitate to you anyway.

The true beauty of Neale Donald Walsch's definition of leadership is that is gives us the freedom and joy to 'go first', to set forth, without feeling the need to have someone follow us. After all, if we have no followers, any expectation of leading someone would leave us feeling adrift. It's our journey so we simply lead ourselves. As the leader of our life, we can choose the paths that suit us, and if others choose to follow, that's fine. If not, that's fine too.

Role Models
The leaders I've had the most appreciation for throughout my life, have been regular people who have also unknowingly been my greatest teachers; those I have learned from simply by observing them as they lead their lives. By following the example they have set when dealing with love, pain, frustration, stress, fear, applause, victory and defeat, I have become a more humble, grounded and loving Being. Without even being aware of it, they encouraged me to follow in their footsteps so that one day I might become a great leader too. What an incredible gift they have shared with me, and most of them don't even know it!

In chapter one I talked about the world's great achievers and it occurs to me that these people are/were also great leaders. Not because they consciously chose to lead others, but because they focused on leading life on their terms, from a place of strength, integrity and joy – and that's an extremely attractive aspect to us. They control their destiny – and we want to do the same.

Whether as employers, team captains, parents, coaches, professional advisors, or any other position of leadership we may find ourselves in, guiding others is a great responsibility – and a great honour. As a parent, I try to lead my son by example and teach him to be compassionate, joyful and accepting of himself and others. I encourage him to dream, to be the best he can be, and to seek out the things that make him feel good. I guide him to look for the positives in every situation and focus on what he wants in his life (as opposed to what he doesn't want). But always, it is up to him to choose to follow my guidance. Sure, as a child he (usually!) does, but it won't always be so. There will come a time when he will choose to follow his own lead, and my job as his caretaker will be done.

My life and career coach (yes, I have one!) is a talented, musical, entrepreneurial spirit; Gilli Moon. I no longer have the intensive level of coaching I once had because Gilli patiently guided me to find my own inner greatness – she taught me to be the leader of my life and she encouraged me to become a coach too. In turn, a number of my coaching clients have gone on to inspire, mentor and coach in their own fields of expertise. I can honestly say it's the most amazing and gratifying feeling to watch a client take flight like that.

I believe the best leaders are the ones who pass on their knowledge and wisdom – they lead us toward the best of who we are and the best of what's inside us, and in the process, teach us how to pass that on to the next wave of people searching for the greatness inside of them. Great leaders inspire more great leaders.

The Unconscious Leader
Most of the time, we lead unintentionally. We go about our daily lives doing what we do - working, helping others, reaching for our dreams, etc – without realising the people around us may be taking note of our actions and behaviour. When we trigger a response inside the heart and mind of someone else, we have a hand in leading them to it. Leadership is a massive responsibility and yet it's one we are often unaware of having.

When the choices we make and the actions we take for ourselves are a catalyst for someone else defining and refining their choices and actions - that is leadership. Yes, it's leading by example, but I think it's even more than that. There is a soul-deep desire within us to emotionally and spiritually nurture, support and create with others. It's the energy-based connection that exists between us that drives us to learn then lead, then learn and lead some more. The process is lifelong, constant and powerful.

We are responsible for leading ourselves toward the joy, love and goals we seek. We are the leader of our own life, but the choices we make can influence others, and that's a responsibility too. Not because we are responsible for the choices and action of others, but because as Soul Beings, we are all connected, so the energy we 'put out there' affects all.

That's why being a conscious leader is so important. By that I mean, we need to be more aware of our own thoughts, behaviours and actions, knowing we may be observed as a role model for, and by, others. Knowing we have the awesome power and capacity to change the world.

And we do.

STATEMENT 11

You alone are responsible for your actions.

The Power In Being Responsible

Every thought, word and action
belongs to you.
You alone are responsible
for your life and
all you give out to the world.
No one else has power
over the choices you make.

You draw to you
all the people and experiences
that are present in your life.
This is the degree of your power,
so great that you can alter
any aspect of your life
that does not serve you.

Embrace your role
as the Creator of that
which pours forth from you,
and remember to remain
solemn and humbled
by the responsibility...

for your power can change the world.

11

This Statement is so obvious, isn't it? We can all read it and on an intellectual level understand the implicit meaning of it. As individuals, we are responsible for everything we think, feel, say and do – and whilst we are not responsible for the reactions of others to what we do, we are responsible for the direct results of our actions. This is such an important and powerful aspect of Being Human. Taking conscious responsibility for our actions gives us the opportunity to think carefully about the consequences to ourselves, our loved ones, and even our community and the world at large.

I'm reminded of Uncle Ben's statement to his young nephew, Peter Parker (aka 'Spiderman'), when he stated "With great power comes great responsibility". I believe the reverse is just as true. When we accept responsibility for our actions we activate immense power - inner strength, confidence, compassion and thoughtful consideration - all incredibly powerful aspects of the Self.

Why then, do so many people try to abdicate responsibility, or act irresponsibly, on a daily basis? It's certainly a fear-based response, but where does it come from? Taking ownership of our actions means we also have to acknowledge our mistakes. And it means we have to acknowledge our triumphs. Both can be equally scary if our self-esteem is low.

I think that accepting responsibility for our actions is an act of humility, which some people confuse with humiliation. Rather than understanding the power to be found in responsibility, they feel afraid they will be seen as weak or stupid. In the case of being commended or applauded, some fear they don't deserve the praise, and worry others will see through them and notice just how weak or stupid they actually are. Either way, for these people, it just seems easier to place responsibility (blame or accolade) on someone or something else. Then perhaps, no one will ever notice their inherent weakness and stupidity. But again, the reverse is true; being responsible for our actions (both mistakes and accomplishments) demonstrates strength and intelligence.

Playing The Blame Game
When we refuse to take responsibility for our actions, we become powerless pawns in the Blame Game. The biggest problem with playing the Blame Game is that you can never win. You'll always walk away feeling you have less power and self-esteem than you started out with. And people who play the Blame Game usually have a lack of inner power and self-esteem to begin with.

As a compulsive, depressed and angry person for many years, I became an expert player of 'The Blame Game'. Whenever something went wrong (which was often, as is the case with people whose lives are out of control) it always seemed to be someone else's fault. Something always stood in my way and stopped me from having what I wanted. To say that I was resentful is an understatement. My internal mantra to the world was "help me or get out of my way". I was the ultimate Blamer.

When I entered the 12 Step program, Overeaters Anonymous, and began to clean up my act, accepting responsibility for my actions was a huge deal. It was also a relief. Accepting responsibility for my actions enabled me, slowly but surely, to take real control in a healthy way for the first time in my life. I'd been 'faking it' for so long that when I began to feel authentic inner power and self-esteem, it was a revelation to me. Since then, I've met many others who have felt the same way.

There are always two points of view, two or more players in the Blame Game. I call them The Blamer and The Target. The Blamer is the person who refuses to take responsibility for anything 'bad' that happens in their lives, and The Target is the poor soul who is expected to take on the burden of The Blamer's actions. A strong and self-contained person rarely gets involved in the Blame Game. They accept responsibility for their actions without the need to find someone to blame, and they would never allow a Blamer to pile their 'stuff' onto them.

Playing the Blame Game is a form of abuse, so if you're involved, even unconsciously, it's time to take charge, take back your power and take responsibility for your actions.

The Blamer
I want you to commit right now to be really honest with yourself and the following questions. This is not a test, there are no points to score, no wrong answers, and there is no punishment or condemnation to avoid.

- Do you often feel that people, circumstances or other outside influences cause problems in your life?

- Do you feel that no matter how hard you try, something always happens to get in the way of your goals, dreams and ultimately, your happiness?

- Do you place the blame for the 'bad stuff' in your life squarely on the shoulders of others or outside influences, knowing they are at fault?

- Has anyone ever suggested that you are unfair, irresponsible, mean or abusive?

I know these questions are confronting but it's okay if you answered yes to any or all of them. If you've been playing the Blame Game for a while, it's tough to look honestly at your life and recognise that, perhaps you've been refusing to accept responsibility for your actions and been blaming everyone and everything around you for the state you're in. If you have answered yes to some or all of the above questions, I want you to know how proud I am of you for being willing to see yourself in an honest and authentic way. This is the beginning of accepting responsibility, and drawing true power, into your life.

It's also the turnaround you've been waiting for. Being responsible for your actions means that you have the power to make your dreams come true. No one else has the power to crush them unless you give it to them. That's right. The only power that others hold over you is the power you give them. When we blame someone else for things that 'go wrong' we are making ourselves the victim. We give away our power, and because we feel powerless, we try to make someone feel more powerless than we are by landing the Blame ball in their court. That's supposed to make us feel better. But no one wins this game.

> *Steve is driving on the highway, miles from anywhere, and the car sputters, jerks and rolls to a stop on the roadside. He looks at the fuel gauge and it's sitting on empty! WTF??? His wife was the last person to drive the car. Why didn't she fill up when she must have seen how low the fuel was? Now Steve is stuck in the middle of nowhere, it's beginning to rain and he's late for an important meeting.*

He calls his wife on his mobile phone and rips into her for her lack of consideration and foresight in not fuelling up yesterday. After a barrage of abuse, Steve hangs up on his poor beloved and tries to phone his motoring service for assistance – but now his phone battery has lost its charge! Disgusted, Steve hurls the phone out the car window just in time for a passing semi- to obliterate it.

Steve's having a CRAP morning. The world is against him today and there's nothing he can do about it.

It's like a scene from a horror movie – or a comedy – and, okay, it sounds a little over the top, but this kind of stress-laden scenario happens every day to a lot of people. Whilst I've never personally had this particular day, I've certainly had similar experiences and maybe you have too. I can cringe about them now, and in doing so, the reality of the above scenario is clear. The only person responsible for Steve's situation is Steve.

Steve didn't check the fuel gauge this morning and fill up. Steve didn't charge his phone battery overnight. Steve used up the little amount of battery charge he had by shouting at his wife on his phone, and Steve had the hissy fit and threw his phone in the path of a truck. Steve is sitting in his immobilised car on the side of the highway, waist deep in his own self-pity and resentment (as his long-suffering wife files for divorce), because he doesn't have his act together, so he blames everyone and everything else for his predicament. And deep down, he probably knows it.

The Target

Just like the questions regarding The Blamer, I want you to commit right now to being really honest with yourself and the following questions. Again, this is not a test, there are no points to score, no wrong answers, and there is no punishment or condemnation to avoid.

- Do you often get blamed for the actions/choices of a loved-one, co-worker, friend or partner?

- Do you ever feel that, in the eyes of someone close to you, you can never 'get anything right'?

- Are you ever told that you are the cause of problems in someone else's life?

- Are you ever told that "it's all your fault"?

Camilla had a great day. She made some good sales at her casual job and the boss noticed. She got the dog to the vet for his shots, picked the kids up from school, grabbed some groceries on the way home and prepared a nice meal for her family. She even got the laundry done while the kids watched some TV. The washing up is done, the kids are bathed and in bed and Steve is on the computer playing White Walkers. Exhausted, Camilla crawls into bed.

The next morning, after the usual hectic rush to get Steve and the kids breakfasted, dressed and off to school and work, Camilla, who has the day off work, puts on her favourite CD and cheerfully starts on the housework. The phone rings. It's her husband.

Camilla's day is about to go south. After listening to a tirade of abuse and trying to calm him down (to no avail) she apologises and starts to suggest he call the motoring service - but he hangs up on her with an angry retort.

Dissolving into tears, Camilla sinks to the floor feeling distressed, humiliated and guilty. For years, she has been Steve's scapegoat when things go wrong. This is the last straw for her and she won't take it anymore. She turns on the computer and Googles 'divorce lawyers'.

Camilla is a classic example of a Target. She gets blamed for things that go wrong for Steve and this makes her feel powerless at times. It got to the point where she felt her only options were to allow the abuse to continue or leave the relationship altogether.

Camilla is lucky in that she has an independent income from work which gives her satisfaction and life skills. She is confident in her role as a mother/nurturer and she's appreciated at work which helps her feel better about herself too. Although her self-esteem is low because of Steve's abuse, she is a fairly cheerful person by nature and she still feels strong enough to make a decision to get out from under the abuse. Some Targets within relationships become so powerless over the course of long-term abuse that they are enslaved in their situations. They are the physically beaten, emotionally battered and/or psychologically scarred results of domestic violence, long-term workplace harassment and schoolyard bullying.

The one thing in common between the Blamer and the Target is that they are both victims; the Blamer is a victim of their inability to see their role in the situation and accept responsibility for it, and the Target is a victim of their inability to stand up for themselves. So how can Steve and Camilla (and we) stop playing the Blame Game?

Stake Your Claim
Keep in mind that the result of every word or action begins with a thought. We manifest everything in our life (whether intentionally or not) so if we can understand the part we've played, we can take responsibility and claim ownership of our actions and choices. We can begin to regain our power.

In order to release the blame on ourselves and others, we first need to remind ourselves of the powerful, non-judgemental and loving Statements of the CUSB. They are designed to help us release all negative and destructive thoughts, feelings and actions. This helps us move into a calm and balanced State internally and allows us to think in a more positive and creative way.

Next, we begin working backward to the original thought that 'started the ball rolling' on the situation at hand. We can start with the question, "How and why did I invite this situation into my life?" Just by asking this question we begin to take responsibility for our role in the situation. We redirect the ball of responsibility from a would-be Target to where it really belongs. Squarely back in our court. This is a process that works in every situation.

To stop playing the Blame Game and start being responsible for our actions, we need to think the way the Universe 'thinks'. The Universe will take note of our core desire and the underlying vibration of the emotional foundation it sits on and deliver exactly based on that. This means we need to be acutely aware of how we are feeling and how we ask for what we want.

You might be in a current situation that you KNOW you didn't ask for, but here's an example based on my own experience:

I lost my job. Who was at fault? The manager could have chosen any employee when the company downsized because of the downturn in the economy, but (of course) she chose me. It was hard enough to keep my head above water with the bills I had. Now I was going to sink faster than a stone in a lily pond.

That's how I felt. Then I thought about how I'd been feeling in the preceding months. I'd spent a lot of time stewing over my manager and how I disliked her. I'd been wishing I could have more time to do the things I loved to do but I was working six days per week in a job I wasn't happy with. I'd been feeling resentful of not earning enough money for the hours I worked and always struggling to pay bills.

Think about it. When our thoughts and desires burst out from us, the Universe will deliver back a precise reflection every time. Hate my job? Want more time for me? Never have enough money? Okay! said the Universe, and it released me from the job, giving me plenty of time for me and reinforcing my emotional foundation of lack. Hey, I asked for it and the Universe delivered!

What have you been asking for? Regardless of your own personal situation, before you go blaming the boss, the company the economy, [insert your target here], think about what you've been focusing on and you'll find that, when it comes right down to it, you are the responsible party.

Whether we want to blame someone else; our spouse, parents, boss, other drivers, terrorists, leaders, God, etc, or blame something else; the economy, the Government, the weather, a rise in crime, global warming, banks, multi-national corporations – the list of blame-worthy people and things is endless. But the list we create is BS. None of these people or things is responsible for us or for what happens to us. We are the creator of our own life, and any part that others play in it is by invitation only.

So, looking again at the scenario above with what I now know, how would I consciously ask for a better job that gives me more time for myself and pays more money into the bargain? Exactly like that:

"I want a job I love, more time for the things I want to do and more income than I get now".

Of course I'd also need to alter my feelings from negative to positive to change my perspective and focus ie;

"The job I have now is paying me the money I need to live on and I really appreciate that. It will see me through until my perfect job comes up. I'm so excited about the future and I'm looking forward to a great new job that gives me more time for me and pays me well. In the meantime, I'm enjoying today and all the abundance it offers me."

Or something like that.

You can apply this way of thinking to any situation and with practice and focus it won't take long to feel happier within yourself, and thus, set yourself up for more positive thoughts, feelings and actions. Eventually, this conscious activity becomes a natural part of who you are and how you think.

Every person, situation and thing that comes into our life is there because we either manifest or allow it. We truly have that kind of power. We alone are responsible for our thoughts, feelings and actions, and for the reactions we have to every situation in our life. Others may be involved because of their own actions or reactions, but that's their path. In the end, we have to be responsible for the path we pave for ourselves and, in a stone at each turn in the road, carve the words *"I was here"*.

STATEMENT 12

You can never make a wrong choice. There are good choices and bad choices, but all choices lead to experiences that cause the expansion of Being.

Making Life Choices is Never Easy

...just know that the Universe supports you
because each choice is perfect.

There are moments in life
when we come to a crossroads,
and we have to make choices
about the course we are to take
as we travel life's journey.

Don't be afraid to
follow your dreams.
They are worthy of your efforts
to achieve them, and
you deserve to make them a reality.

I believe in you.
You really do have the capacity for
courage, strength and determination,
so trust in yourself and your ability
to make the decisions
that are right for you.

Above all,
make the choices that
will give you ultimate joy
and fulfilment,
because then you will know that
regardless of the challenges ahead

...you have chosen the right path.

12

My Story

I looked down at the bottle of pills in my hand and wondered idly if they would cause me pain before they killed me. Taken as directed, they were pain killers. I shook the bottle. It was almost full, so, nearly fifty pills.

Surely enough to kill my pan.

I'd endured seventeen years of being bullied and beaten, feeling despised, worthless, unprotected and defenceless. I'd reached the end of my capacity for pain. Any physical torture the pills might cause would just be life's last "hurrah". Life was all about agony of one sort or another so I expected no less from my last hours. I didn't care anymore - I'd had enough.

I sat on the edge of my bed and swallowed the pills a few at a time, washing them down with water, until the bottle was empty. I lay down and closed my eyes with no regret that I wouldn't be opening them again. I was alone in the house for the next few days. So I knew I wouldn't be disturbed. No one was going to save me. There was nothing left to save anyway.

I was exhausted, as only a person suffering with severe depression can be exhausted. If you've been there you know what I mean. It's like all the life force has been sucked out of you and you're left with no energy, no feeling, no spirit, no hope. Nothing but nothing. Death with a heartbeat.

So what about the pain? That wasn't 'nothing'. I think I'd gone so far beyond caring that the depression kicked in and smothered it.

I lay on the bed. Tears of deep sadness and loneliness trickled from under my closed lids, down my temples and washed through my hair to melt into the pillow. Relief and peace washed through my body and melted into my soul.

Finally, it was over. I would be free.

I was seventeen years old when I chose to die. I had no romantic notions of last minute rescue and I didn't care if there was anything – or nothing - beyond death. I felt a total withdrawal into myself with no thought other than the absolute certainty that I couldn't continue to live in the bottomless abyss of my emotional and psychological pain.

To my mind at that time, nothing mattered but to end the misery. There was no thought of the impact my death would have on others. I had completely retreated into myself. Some say suicide is a selfish act. I can only speak from my own experience in saying that for me, it was 100% an attempt to release myself from genuine emotional suffering and psychological torment. It was an act of seeking relief, even a form of self-preservation, from the soul's point of view.

Selfish? Maybe to those who didn't know me well enough to understand just how hard I'd tried to fit in, to be accepted, to find my place; to be happy. But the people who knew me and loved me - I think they would have been deeply saddened but understanding of my actions. One doesn't suicide to hurt others. One suicides to relieve one's own hurt.

Obviously my suicide attempt failed.

I woke about twelve hours later and whilst nothing had changed - everything had changed. I remember lying there on the bed feeling confused at first. Why hadn't I died like I was supposed to? A thought whispered through me: Because it's not time for you to die now. There is something more you have to do.

In that crucial moment, I was given a reason to live. There was something I still had to do; A mission, something I was required to accomplish. It appeared I still had usefulness.

Hope surged through me even though I had no idea what that 'something' was or how I could even begin to find it. All I know is, in that moment I felt God had decided to thwart my suicide effort and keep me here for a specific purpose. I chose to accept that and try to figure out what that 'something' was so my life could be better, worthwhile, justified. I've been trying to figure that out ever since. Of course, now I recognise that I don't have to justify myself. I don't need to prove my worthiness. I am a perfectly imperfect piece of God and like every other being, I have a right to be here and I have a right to be happy.

Why have I included my suicide experience in this chapter? Because I look at the choice I made to end my life and I can't fathom it as being a 'wrong' choice. I even find it challenging to mark it as either a bad or a good choice. It was simply the choice I made at that time befitting of my desire to end my miserable experience here on earth. As it turns out, the result of my choice has been as inspiring as it was unexpected. It has added to my life experience and impacted every State of my Being.

Of course, it is incredibly sad that anyone would feel so deeply distressed - so utterly broken, worthless and unlovable - that they would willingly take steps to end their life. But I feel so much appreciation that I had that experience. So many positives have come out if it. I have a greater capacity for compassion, empathy and understanding, a deeper insight into the thoughts and feelings of others, and it's given me intuitive awareness of when depression is present, not just in myself but also in others.

Mis-takes
We can learn from every experience regardless of whether we perceive it to be a good or bad one – in fact, I believe we learn more, and can be most positively influenced by, the 'bad' choices. There is an art in being able to review our 'mistakes' without attachment so we can learn from them without being ruled forever by guilt, shame, resentment or fear.

If you were to ask a movie director for their definition of a mis-take they would tell you it was simply a line or a scene that was acted out in a way that the director found unappealing and therefore needed to be reshot (acted out again).

We are each the director, the actor and the script writer of our own life. With so many choices, so many options for actions available to us every day, we are sure to enact the occasional mis-take. It seems to me that the most reasonable response is to mentally yell "Cut!" and next time enact a different choice. Eventually we will be happy with the result of the 'scene' (scenario) and the 'take' will be 'in the can'.

Of course, we can't always go back immediately and choose again, much as we'd often like to. Sometimes we (and others) have to live with the mis-takes we make, and that's when we have to practice self-forgiveness and honesty and reparation with those who have been affected by our choice. Take responsibility for it, sort it out and move on. I guarantee that at some point, the same situation will occur again; it's the Universe's gift - an opportunity to choose again, to call "Action!", and try for a more appealing outcome. Okay, enough of the movie-making analogy.

Choices, Outcomes and Reactions
I think it is really important to carefully consider this constitutional statement and its true meaning. It's not about refusing to take responsibility for screwing up, nor is it about excusing bad behaviour or a crime. It's about accepting the consequences of our actions but not being torn down by them.

Choices allow us a wide variety of life experiences so why look back at them and mark them as having been right or wrong, good or bad? Sure, we all make choices that result in experiences we'd rather not go through, but even these are a means of growth, of personal and Universal evolution.

We learn so much from every choice we make. Not only do we learn to make choices we are happy with, we get better at making all our choices work for us, regardless of the outcomes. Because how we react to the outcomes of our choices is a choice we make. This is one of the most profound revelations I've had in my life so it's worth repeating:

How we react to the outcomes of our choices is a choice we make.

I can choose to feel completely devastated by the outcome of a choice I've made, or I can choose to appreciate the outcome as a lesson well-learned, a means to making better choices in future, even a gift from God. I can choose to feel either 'less' or 'blessed' because of the experience. And so can you.

It's not always easy to choose a positive response to a 'bad' choice we've made. Often our thoughts (followed swiftly by our emotions) move into auto-response mode and we feel guilty, self-critical, even stupid for making the choice that landed us in hot water. This is where managing our reaction becomes crucial and it requires the rewiring of our brain by consciously altering our habitual thoughts.

Reversal of Thought
For me, the process of rewiring involves my willingness to find the blessings, the positives that can be found in any situation. I call it Reversal of Thought. When something goes 'wrong', I feel the initial negative reaction or emotion rise up inside and immediately begin to look for the aspects of the situation that make me feel better.

For example, when a relationship ends there can be all sorts of negative emotions floating around from anger and betrayal (s/he said they would love me forever), guilt/ regret (I must have done something wrong), to feeling unloved, used and abandoned (I've wasted all these years and now I'm alone and too old to find love again and who'd want me anyway?). Not to mention the stress of legal issues such as divorce, property division, custody of the kids, etc. It's probably the most common of all the stressful and heartbreaking experiences we can go through.

With any situation, the thing to remember is that everyone wants an outcome that will lead them to feel happier. When a relationship has broken down and it's time to move on, staying calm, making choices and decisions that are love-based rather than steeped in hate or vindictiveness will make the whole process of separation as painless as possible for yourself, your kids, and yes, your partner. Rather than focusing on legal struggles, 'winning' or fear of losing out, focus on feeling secure in the knowledge that no harm can come to you, you will always have everything you need, you are perfect, eternal and loveable and nothing can change that – and every experience leads to personal growth and the expansion of Being.

We can use Reversal of Thought in any situation where we want to alter our negative perception to find a happier feeling and a more positive outlook. Basically, if we can feel better, we can feel calmer and when we're calmer, we can think more clearly. At that point we have the opportunity to come to terms with the situation as it is and feel okay about it or we can start working toward positive thought or action that will improve the situation. Either way, we move forward. We are causing the evolvement of our Being.

At best, a 'bad' choice is not the end of the world. At worst, a bad choice is not the end of the world. Really. Unless you have the responsibility of a thousand nuclear warheads and the little red button at your disposal, no mistake you make is unrecoverable. We can't bring back a life we take away - there are some outcomes to choices we can never reverse, but we needn't allow any choice we make to have absolute power over us forever. We have the right to make amends where we can, to forgive ourselves, to allow ourselves to heal, and to have the opportunity to do better next time.

How we react to outside forces, is also a choice we make. We can't control the actions of others - or any force outside of our self. In situations where we find ourselves caught up in the maelstrom of someone or something else's actions, often the only thing we do have control over is how we choose to react emotionally, physically and psychologically.

Learning to cope with everything that is thrown at us is a skill I'm still trying to master. Mostly, I cope pretty well these days when facing the dramas of life, though I admit to still having a 'hissy fit' at bad drivers when I'm on the road! My young son then turns to me and suggests it might be time for me to take my 'happy pills' (naturopathic remedies I take for stress and anxiety – I highly recommend them!). Children are such levellers, eh? ☺

I've found that the key to a fast recovery, when we find ourselves in these less than ideal situations, is to take a step back and breathe. I have to force myself not to react immediately in these situations, but rather, to stop and gain some emotional distance. If I can do this, I'm giving my Emotional Self time to regain balance and my Psychological Self space to calmly implement Reversal of Thought. This may seem like I'm counteracting my instinct for fight or flight, but most of the situations we find ourselves in, in this modern age, provide neither fight nor flight conditions, so a more thoughtful reaction is likely to be appropriate.

There are always positive aspects, silver linings, and reasons for appreciation to be found in every situation. With practice, Reversal of Thought becomes a valuable tool that can turn any situation into a constructive experience.

Understanding that we have freedom of choice is something only the human species has. We have evolved beyond unconscious acts based on primal instinct and expanded to a point where conscious choice has become a part of our everyday lives. This Statement compels us to evolve further. It asks us to understand that the choices we make can never hold us separate from the perfection that is inherent within us. It reminds us that choice is simply an opportunity to further expand our Being.

STATEMENT 13

As you journey along your life's path, don't be afraid to step off it occasionally. There is much beauty to be found on the side of the road, and new experiences to discover. The discoveries on these side journeys will help you further 'down the track'.

Your dreams are just a step away...

Every journey, whether short or long,
must be taken step by step
with patience and persistence
and a clear sense of direction.
Each path offers another opportunity
to grow and learn
and become more than you are now.

It's in the act of travelling that you learn
the resilience needed to continue on.
It doesn't matter how long it takes -
each moment is precious,
and every experience is valuable.
So as you travel on,
remember to enjoy the scenery
along the path of every day.

When you feel inspired
to try something new,
don't be afraid to explore new paths
for they are part of your journey too,
and much can be learned from
the experiences they hold.

The joy and satisfaction
of reaching your destination
is always in the journey
you are taking to reach it,
so focus on each moment,
each step, and know
you will get there in the end.

13

Have you ever experienced an unexpected event that takes you in a completely different direction to the one you were on – and it's life-changing? I have! I admit that I've never been afraid to step off the main path and explore other avenues. I think it's the 'creative' in me. I don't feel bound to one way of creating – and life is all about creativity.

The last chapter talked about choices and how they are never wrong, so choosing a different direction or setting something aside to try something new can't be a bad thing. It doesn't mean we were heading in the wrong direction or that we can't make up our minds (though it can seem that way at times!). Changing direction and trying something new is a courageous and freedom-loving act. It means that we want to expand our lives and nourish our soul with new experiences. It means we are not afraid to follow our ever-evolving needs and desires.

Though attitudes are changing now, for generations it was regarded as the acceptable thing to learn a trade and then work in that trade for the rest of your career. To change your mind and do something else five, ten or twenty years later was considered absurd. Of course, women were mostly home makers back then and so were labelled as 'flighty' or perhaps 'tomboys' if they chose to do something other than be a housewife and mother. Men, being the primary bread winners, were considered irresponsible if they decided to return to study, change careers or heaven forbid, enter the Arts!

The term 'mid-life crisis' is a classic example of how society has regarded the change of heart, the expansion of mind and the desire for a new and different experience that often occurs in our forties and fifties. 'Mid-life' is like a coming of age, when we begin to gain a deeper understanding of who we are and what we want in relationship to the world and the people around us. It's a yearning for the return of the freedom and joy we felt (or wanted to feel) as children, the desire to make unrepentant, unfettered choices for ourselves regardless of what others may think.

Some of us are lucky. We understand our right to change our minds, make new choices and alter our life's direction well before we hit middle age. I'm one of those people. I've always felt the desire to try new things, though I remember once staying in a job I hated for six years. I felt compelled to stay for the regular pay packet but I was beyond miserable and my health, well-being and behaviour suffered as a result. It was soul-destroying for me and I became very depressed. When I finally moved on it was like life was breathed into me for the first time in years. I'll never stay in a job past its 'use by' date again.

Sight-Seeing
Being a life-long 'sight-seer' has been a blessing for me. There really is so much to take in as we travel through life and believe me, each altered path, each new direction, provides information that is vital knowledge waiting to be used at a future time. I love coming across a 'fork in the road' and exploring the opportunities that lie on new paths.

We are creating every second, with our thoughts, our words and our actions. We create with our dreams and with our hearts. We all express our creativity in different ways and using many outlets. Some are artistic, or they create through gardening, cooking, computer programing, accounting, healing, motivating and inspiring others, making others feel better with a smile or kind word – every thought, every action is creative.

So when you take a new path in your life journey, it is just another way of expressing your creativity. Changing your mind really means you are being drawn to create something new. Exploring other activities other than the one you are primarily occupied with, means you are discovering a new aspect of your creativity. That's why we have 'hobbies'. That's why we go on holidays, and it's why we are fascinated with the lives of others.

Our desire to learn, experience and evolve compels us to explore outside the boundaries of our current situation. It inspires us to discover the variety found on the side of the road, or the entirely different view found on a side track. I love being 'side-tracked'!

Desires -V- Obligations
For some people, it feels extremely hard to step out in a different direction. I've noticed over the years, when clients are feeling directionless, or they feel stuck in dead-end job or unable to move forward, it's often because they are afraid to step off the path they are on. When I ask them what they love doing (or would love to do), it often turns out to be something they feel is outside their capacity to achieve or its far beyond consideration because it doesn't match their current circumstances or fit in with their job or family commitments.

The feeling of obligation to others is a big roadblock for a lot of people, but it doesn't need to be that way. Putting aside for one moment, my belief that we are truly only ever obligated to ourselves, there are ways to follow those exciting, beckoning side paths we feel passionate about and still fulfil those perceived obligations to others.

Start by setting aside a block of time each week to begin exploring that new path as a hobby. Maybe there are other people in your town who enjoy the same pursuit with whom you can spend time. Perhaps there are regular meetings or gatherings you can attend. Can you do some weekend volunteering for 'hands on' experience? Is there a night course or some form of external college course you can do in your own time, around your obligations? If you want to make something, say, wood carved toys, jewellery, pottery or pasta sauce etc, can you have a stall at a local market or fair where you can sell your product and create an income from your hobby? Start thinking outside the box and you'll come up with ways to indulge in your passion whilst still maintaining your family and work commitments. If it's something you can involve your family in (assuming they are willing!) you could end up having, not only a wonderful bonding experience, but perhaps a thriving family business that you love!

I know you might be thinking, *"It's easier said than done."* You're right. If it were easy, you'd already be doing it! My questions for you are: *"What are you afraid of? What do you think is at risk? Will you regret not following your heart's desire?"*

The great thing about following a new path as a hobby is you're not risking anything. You're indulging in your desire to try something new and it doesn't have a negative impact on other commitments. At the same time, you are being true to yourself and allowing something special into your life.

I think the thing to remember is that you can't get it wrong. Regardless of the paths you travel on, you'll always end up at the right place in the end. It's a bit like being in the supermarket. You wander up and down the aisles picking out the things on your shopping list and suddenly you think you'd really like fruit salad for desert tonight. So you head back to the 'Fruit and Veg' section and pick out the fruit you want. While you're doing that you think, "Hmmm. Fresh cream would be perfect with the fruit salad." So you cross back to the 'Dairy' aisle. Then you remember you used the last of the coffee this morning and didn't add it to the list, so you make your way over to 'Beverages'. You crisscross the store to meet your desires, never thinking to yourself "What if I get lost?" Regardless of which aisles you go down, you know you'll end up at the check outs!

Like the supermarket, in life, you can choose whatever you want, or choose your reactions to the experiences placed before you, and you will always end up where you are supposed to be.

Changes in the Scenery
Of course, we can be perfectly happy on the path we are on and with the people and experiences we find on it – and then something changes and suddenly it all seems to go awry. Why does that happen?

As we choose each path along our journey we change and grow with the new experiences we have. As a result, not only do we change internally through our altered thoughts and desires, but our relationships, preferences and other external experiences are altered too. We are drawn to people, places and activities that encompass, embrace and reflect the path we are on.

Sometimes we can feel side-tracked by forces outside our control, but we can learn to deal with every change, every transition, by trusting in ourselves, using our intuition and setting our fear aside. Change is just change. How we deal with it is the difference between moving forward on our journey or being immobilised by a roadblock of our own making.

Transition on the path can be subtle or dramatic, but either way, if you're not sure if you are on the best path, take a look at the external qualities of your life and how you feel about them. They are a reflection of the path you are on, so if the people and activities in your life create a feeling of joy, self-worth and appreciation within, you know you're on the 'right track'. If you feel uncomfortable, stressed, resentful or powerless – or just plain restless, it might be time to try a different path and some new scenery.

Travelling with Soul Mates
One enormous challenge we face on our journey is when things change between soul mates.

We connect with soul mates throughout our life, sometimes for a day, sometimes for a lifetime. I believe that soul mates are those Beings with whom we have made an agreement before coming into this physical life, to bring about experiences that will help us to grow and evolve. Soul mates come into our life in the form of siblings, parents, lovers, abusers, friends, teachers, strangers - even pets. We connect with many soul mates throughout our physical lifetime.

When we have a close, loving bond with a soul mate and we travel together on a path, it's truly life-changing. There is immense joy and exhilaration in connecting with someone who encourages the best in us, who loves and supports us unconditionally and vice versa, and with whom we have a mutual appreciation and understanding. It is perhaps the most intensely beautiful and wondrous experience we can have.

The thing is, even though it may seem that we are on the same path as a soul mate, it really only seems that way. The truth is, we are all on our own independent paths. Those paths sometimes connect and give us the opportunity to walk together for a while until going their individual ways again. When those paths separate, it can feel like a devastating loss, as though a significant, if not essential, part of us is suddenly missing.

This happened to me recently, when the loss of a beloved soul mate almost toppled me, leaving in its wake the sensation of a painful, gaping hole in my chest and my life. I thought he would be an integral part of my world forever so when that changed I was left feeling bereft and broken.

When the paths of soul mates move in different directions it can be heartbreaking and confusing. Weren't we meant to be together forever? The answer seems to be "*No*". But the truth is we can never really lose a soul mate. As well as taking into account the Soul Connection that exists between every single one of us, the experiences that soul mates share on the paths of their physical lives often change them irrevocably, and they each leave the other with a portion of their essence that can never be erased. Soul mates truly are with us forever – in our hearts and in the expression of who we've become because of them, so they are never lost to us, even after they have left our physical space.

There are some soul mates we are glad to see the backs of; the ones who taught us to understand what we don't want in our lives! But if we can utilise what we learned in Chapter 6 and appreciate the experience they brought to us, we can also appreciate and forgive the abusive soul mate. After all, they provided us with growth and greater understanding of ourselves and others. They too leave their essence, but we can choose how we feel about that and appreciate them for what they have taught us. They are a valuable part of our journey too.

The Destination
Side paths can be just that - leisurely detours. Sometimes the path widens out and we find ourselves on a completely different journey than the one we started out on and that's fine too. As this Statement of the Constitution suggests, all paths lead to new experiences – and those experiences are destined to both teach and enthral.

The destination is only important in that, as human beings, it's our nature to need something to work toward. If our desires, our end goals, the destination, changes - that's okay. It shows the evolution of our Self, that we are capable of changing our minds, switching paths, to best suit our needs in the moment. That's why our focus on the journey is of far greater importance. Awareness of each moment and feeling happy, excited and appreciative in it, is the best destination anyone could wish for don't you think?

STATEMENT 14

At all times, remember to honour and respect your Self. Enjoy your Self and be excited about the life you've been given.

You Deserve the Best of Everything...

This world has so much to offer,
and there are so many beautiful experiences,
people and places awaiting you.
So enjoy your Self and
ask for nothing less
than you know you deserve.

You are worthy of respect
and you honour yourself
when you stand up for
your right to receive it.
You have the right to be happy,
to be joyful and free
and to care for your well-being.

We are given that
which we give out
So honour and respect yourself
and all those around you
for we are but reflections of each other
as we co-exist
connected through Soul Energy.

14

This Statement relates closely to Statement #7; 'Be loving and kind to yourself and you will find it easier to be loving and kind to others'. There is a difference though. In Chapter 7 we looked at how we can nurture ourselves from an emotional or 'heartfelt' point of view. In this chapter we look at how we can nurture ourselves from an intellectual or 'mindful' point of view.

What does it mean to honour and respect ourselves? How do we quantify that? Among other things, it means protecting and nurturing our self-esteem and self-worth. It means standing firm in our expectation of others to respect our rights and needs. It means that we insist upon a level of conduct from ourselves toward our Self that reflects the level of honour and respect we desire.

Saying "No" Is Never Easy
If you're a 'people-pleaser' like me, you'll really relate to this. How often do you say "Yes" to people when you really want to scream "No"? Well, screaming aside, it's really unhealthy and disrespectful to our Self to constantly put the wants and needs of others ahead of our own. It makes us feel resentful, frustrated, used and emotionally exhausted. So, why do we do it?

I became a people-pleaser at a very young age. I wanted to please my mother because I sensed her unhappiness with her life, my father so he wouldn't fly into a rage, the kids at school in the hope they would stop bullying me – and everyone else in the hope they would see past whatever dreadful flaws I'd apparently been born with, and like me anyway.

As I grew to adulthood, I attracted people into my experience who took advantage of my people-pleasing nature, but even though I often felt resentful that the balance of give-and-take was way off, I continued to make myself available to others and whatever they needed or wanted from me. Family, friends, colleagues, bosses, lovers – you name it. If they wanted something, I was right there giving it to them.

If this sounds like you, you're not alone. Women are particularly prone to people-pleasing because we are the carers, the nurturers, but men can also fall into this self-defeating activity – especially at work. Climbing the career ladder has its own set of challenges to face; feeling pressured to work back late or on weekends, accepting on short notice a business trip that could earn you a promotion but will mean you'll miss your sister-in-law's wedding, or missing Junior's school play to attend an important business function that you know will earn you 'brownie points' with the company.

What are we really doing when we constantly say *"yes"* to people? We are digging a hole for our self-esteem, our self-respect and our peace of mind because we can never completely please another person. We can die trying though; people-pleasing leads to anger and resentment, and we've already discussed what that can do to us physically and emotionally in chapter 6.

Here's my rule: I put my needs first, then the needs of my son, then the rest of my family, then friends and then everyone else. So I'm going to have to say "no" to someone at some point. Suck it up.

Technically, 'no' is not harder to say that 'yes'. Both words are of the same syllable length and have a definite, unmistakeable meaning that is easily understood in most languages.

You can say no in a gentle but firm way:

"Thanks for asking but I'm already committed on that day. Maybe next time?"

"I appreciate the opportunity for extra hours but I have family plans for that evening. Thank you for asking me though."

"I'd love to help but I already have plans."

Some people (the ones who are used to getting their way with you) might push you to explain yourself, as though whatever your plans are, they can't possibly be more important than helping them. It's your choice whether you elaborate but if you do, be polite but firm. Yes, Junior's school play IS more important to you (and to Junior) than plying a client with drinks that evening to win the contract. Yes, taking a picnic lunch and your favourite Jane Austin novel to the river for restful 'alone time' this Saturday IS more important to you (and your Being) than minding your friend's kids while they go shopping.

'No' is not a dirty word. Next time you feel pressured to say yes when you don't really want to, try "No" on for size. It does take practice, but like everything else, practice makes perfect – and you'll feel lighter and happier knowing you are honouring your needs and showing yourself a higher level of respect.

Show Me The Money!
When we place appropriate financial and emotional value on ourselves and everything we do, it is an outward statement of our inner self-worth.

If you know you're being underpaid for the work you do, approach the boss about a pay rise. Not more hours to make more money. More money per hour. You are allowed to make this request, and if you get the raise – great. If you don't get the raise you know you deserve, perhaps it's time to start looking for a job somewhere else that will pay you what you are worth.

If you work for yourself, set your prices and stick to them. Friends, family and colleagues will constantly expect 'freebies' or discounts. It's up to you whether you choose to give them, but remember; each time you accept less than your set price, you will have to find that money somewhere else if the electricity/phone/rent/food bill is going to get paid. As a small business owner I understand that your business is more than your livelihood. It is your whole life and you pour your heart and soul into it. It's reasonable to expect your customers to value and respect that by paying the appropriate prices for your products/services.

That doesn't mean you should never give freebies or discounts – but make the most of them by using them in Special Offers ('buy two and get the third one free' or 'buy bulk and receive a % discount' or 'the first five bookings get an extra 'widget'' etc) and always run them for a limited time with a set end date. Tell your friends and family about the Special Offer so they can take advantage, and promote, promote, promote! In this way you can keep family and friends happy, perhaps pick up some extra customers and keep control of your budget.

If someone wants to barter products or services with you, make sure that the worth of the barter is equal on both sides, ie; you are getting the exact value in services returned as those you are offering – and only barter for products and services you would normally buy or want anyway.

Point That Thing Someplace Else!
'That Thing' is unacceptable behaviour. Honouring and respecting ourselves means not tolerating unacceptable behaviour toward us from others. This includes finger-pointing (unwarranted blame), destructive opinions, belittling of our dreams and goals, unwanted advice, attempted

physical or emotional coercion or threat, hurtful words and downright rudeness!

If you feel really good about yourself and you show love and kindness toward yourself and others, it stands to reason that you will also have a high level of self-respect and be an honourable person. Honouring and respecting ourselves means being consciously aware of what we are prepared to accept - and not accept – in our life. Whether at work, at school, in the home or in social situations, knowing our worth, and not allowing ourselves or anyone else to undermine it, is vital.

I had a friend of many years who was quite a bit older than me and I looked up to her like a mother or aunt. As she got older, she became resentful, bitter and negative to the point where those feelings saturated everything she said. For a number of years I put up with her hurtful jibes about the work I was doing (or not doing, in her opinion) and discouraging words about my career and creative goals. She constantly questioned everything I did. A coffee visit felt more like an interrogation. It was awful. I'd sit there with a plastic smile on my face while she trampled all over my feelings and my dreams. Nothing seemed to please her, and eventually her criticism and bitterness toward everything and everyone became too overwhelming for me.

I stopped making contact with her and if she did call demanding to know why I hadn't been in contact, I made the excuse that I'd been busy and would stop by in the next few weeks. I never did. I was always too afraid of confrontation to tell her the real reason for my absence. Even in those short calls she would still question me about personal aspects of my life - and always in her demanding, hyper-critical way that made me feel like I was being questioned by the Prosecution! Every contact with her left me feeling 'less than'.

It was a relief when she stopped calling me because I don't want to have to tell her the truth. But I hope that now, if I were to bump into her on the street, I would have the courage to tell her why I've not been in contact. Maybe I could, but then again...

When we are faced with someone's negative behaviour or opinions we have a choice; we can allow it to impact us in a negative way ie; allow them to make our life a misery, or we can shake off our fear and insist they treat us in a more respectful way or take their unacceptable behaviour someplace else. As for the above situation, I suppose I'm sitting somewhere in the middle. No longer prepared to accept the bad behaviour but not yet courageous enough to confront the issue head-on and be honest with my former friend. I'll let you know if that changes!

Sex
Human beings are, to my knowledge, the only physical beings on the planet who use sex for reasons other than simply the continuation of the species. Our brain function is the most highly evolved and we are the only animal species with awareness of Self, though perhaps this trait may also be found to a degree in apes, dolphins and whales. Awareness of Self includes the knowledge and understanding that we are a living Being and that someday we will 'die'. Most animal species are aware of only basic survival – with instincts that drive them to hunt for food, procreate and protect their young. They have no understanding of physical death. Awareness of Self as experienced by human beings is unique to our species.

Perhaps our belief that physical death is 'the end' is the reason why we have developed intense emotion, that we try so hard to fit as many experiences as possible into a few short decades. Our emotional well-being has become closely associated with physical pleasure and our need for connection with each other at every level. I'm certainly not an expert in these things, but it occurs to me that whilst there are many reasons why we have developed so differently from other animals, our knowledge of our impending physical death has to be a driving force in the development of our emotions and desire for understanding of life other than simply 'we live and then we die'.

Perhaps this is why we link sex with more than continuation of the species. It feels good, and pleasure is important to us, and it allows us to connect with each other in every way. What does all this have to do with honouring and respecting ourselves?

I believe that, whether it's performed to have children, as an expression of love or just for fun, sex is supposed be a natural, pleasurable and beautiful part of adult life. It's a physically, emotionally and often spiritually intimate act, so it's important that we protect our self-respect by being sure that we feel happy and comfortable with anyone we have sex with. Having sex with someone when we don't want to, or because we want them to like us, or we think it will somehow gain us power, places our sense of self-worth on a very slippery slope.

Having been in all the above situations, I can say that, for me, the only great sex has been when my whole heart has been in it. Nowadays I can't even imagine having sex with someone I didn't love. I believe that our physical body is the temple of our higher Soul Self, so using it for reasons other than for joyful and loving purposes doesn't make sense to me.

Sex is a touchy subject (pardon the pun!) and I'm not trying to preach here. As with all the notions in this book, this is how I feel. You have to make your own decisions about how you understand and utilise the CUSB Statements but if my thoughts ring true for you, at least consider them and if any of it feels right for you try some of the suggestions on for size.

Are We Having Fun Yet?
I believe life is meant to be enjoyed, that it's supposed to be exciting and filled with experiences that delight and enthral us. When we live our life from a place of honour and respect –

for ourselves and others – we are enjoying a high level of self-esteem, self-love and a commitment to expanding and evolving beyond anything which we, as individuals, as a species, and as One in our Soul-Energy entirety, have ever been before. There is so much joy in the discovery and nurturing of Self. From each experience there is an opportunity to manifest personal, positive growth and understanding of ourselves and the world around us.

Whether you believe that you only have one life to live or that you reincarnate through many, this is the one you're living right now so nurture, honour and respect it and you can experience the excitement of a life led in joy and freedom.

STATEMENT 15

*You are both the Clay and the Potter.
Delight in your changes, growth
and Power.*

The Power Within

You have come into this world
filled with beauty, light and perfection.
Abundance, creativity and love
are already part of who you are
- you are truly a spiritual Being,
borne of the Universe.

You are not separate from God.
You are a loving aspect of that
which is the source of all creation,
the Universal power,
the God you feel in your heart.

As you allow yourself to accept
the true nature of your power,
and you apply it in your physical reality,
you will see miracles occur,
and everything your heart desires
will come to you.

You are the creator and the created
of everything in your life,
and you can achieve great things
with the power that is yours.

15

Of all the Constitution Statements, this is my favourite. I don't believe that God is 'up there' and we are 'down here'. I don't believe that we are separated from God because of mankind's sin or physicality or 'humanness' or anything else. I believe we are each an individual aspect of God, a part of the Universal God Force, an infinite expression of All That Is. Both non-physical and physical, we are the Creative Thought and the Physical Means through which we can be creative. The Potter and the Clay. We are God in perpetual evolution.

Going beyond the notion of 'free will', this statement alludes to the absolute and flawless role we each play in the constant creation, expansion and evolution of All That Is. Although we are inexorably involved in it, I believe that our willing and proactive participation in the process of creation is the greatest gift of joy we can ever give to ourselves and others.

In the Christian religion I grew up in, we were taught that God exists as the Father, the Son and the Holy Spirit. I remember how, in Bible study, water was used as an analogy to explain how God could be three things all at once, because water too, exists in three states: liquid (fluid), steam (gaseous) and ice (solid).

We, too, exist in three major States: body (physical), mind (emotional/psychological) and soul (spiritual). In each case, the three exist as individual aspects of the same thing.

Father	Liquid	Mind	Super Conscious
Son	Solid	Body	Conscious
Holy Spirit	Gas	Soul	Sub Conscious

For me, this explains our ability to be the clay and the potter, the creator and that which we create, and it's a truly awesome concept. It gives us free reign over our choices, our desires - our very future. As God/Universal Energy/All That Is, we have the ability to design our life.

By utilising energy in all three major aspects or States of our Being we bring the Law of Attraction to life. Only we Humans can do this because only we have all the necessary means. In order to activate the Law of Attraction, a Thought must occur in the Mind, then a Desire must be born in the Soul, and then an Action must take place with the Body. Little wonder that God Energy would seek to create Itself in the perfection of the Human experience!

Understanding Our True Power
We are DNA strands of the Universe. That's a powerful statement in itself. We are the thought and the action, the building blocks and the builder, the clay and the potter.

What an amazing feeling – to have such absolute authority over our life and how we choose to live it. It means we can accomplish anything and we have the power to choose everything we want in our lives – right now! It sounds so easy, and it is, if we can get our heads around the enormity of it. Sometimes I wonder if our brains are physically capable of fully absorbing and understanding just what we are equipped for – and yet it is our unique intellectuality that allows us to do exactly that.

We hold ourselves back just because it seems almost beyond our capacity to comprehend how absolute our power is. Yet, in this time of global – even Universal – change, we Humans are increasingly walking a journey of self-discovery and awareness that is allowing us to recognise the truth about our inherent perfection. We are God connecting, evolving and growing ever more beautiful, compassionate and powerful.

You, me, God, tree, star, thought, clay, wheel, potter – it's all the same thing. We are made from the same stuff and we are connected by the same stuff; energy. Energy is, by its very nature, perfect, and as we are 100% energy, we too are perfect.

The Origin Of Thought

The really cool aspect of being Human is our brain. I see our brain as being the 'imperfect' aspect of us. From our brains come thought, emotion, ideas, logic, interpretation, judgement, creativity and decision-making. It is in these brain-originated variables (and there are currently around 7 billion of them) that the beauty and wonder of our imperfection and imagination exists.

The brain is something of an enigma to us. Even with everything we know about the human body and how it works, our most powerful organ, the engine of our vehicle, is still a mystery. We know that we use only a fraction of its capacity and it gives us the ability to communicate and function autonomously and intelligently.

Think about it. Everything Humans have created, from the wheel to air travel, from the telephone to the internet, from penicillin to the atom bomb, has been created from the mind. Thought, imagination and self-belief are powerful tools. It all manifests from the grey matter between our ears and we don't really know how that happens.

We have isolated the different areas of the brain that allow our bodies to perform a wide variety of functions. We understand the connection between the brain and the physical actions of the body. Humans have invented machines that can identify and monitor the brain's electrical impulses - but we still don't understand the origin of thought. What is a thought made of? We know what a thought is and what causes it – we can even watch a thought occur in the brain with the use of computers, but I can't find any research that factually explains what a thought is composed of.

Like many, I believe that thought is pure energy, like the Soul or Spirit. If that's the case, could the origin of thought be borne of our God-self? Perhaps I'm being naïve and my complete lack of scientific knowledge is probably glaringly obvious, but that's okay. I like the idea of our thoughts being linked directly to that aspect of our Self that is God. It has been said that with our thoughts we can change the world. If our thoughts originate from pure energy- God Force - it truly does mean that we have the power, not only to effect change, but to create and achieve anything.

The Double-Edge Of Desire
Why do we have a desire to want things? What creates our feelings of desire? Perhaps we unconsciously feel lacking due to our imperfection. Either way, there seem to be two types of desire; one created from a need for security, and one created from the aspiration to be 'more than'.

I've been deliberate in my choice of words because to me, need leads to a place of fear and aspiration leads to a place of freedom. I believe that the feeling of a lack of security is a disempowering delusion because we are infinite and perfect, and in truth, as both the clay and the Potter, we have (or can create) everything we require for our physical comfort and well-being.

Our desire to be more, to do more and to create more, stems from our Soul/God Self. We understand (albeit unconsciously) that we are constantly evolving and as such we crave new experiences and challenges in order to maintain our infinite evolutionary journey. We love to have goals and dreams – and we feel immense power, joy and satisfaction in reaching them – but if we hold ourselves apart from these joyful experiences, we feel disappointment and even despair.

Advertisers understand the two types of desire and play on them for all they're worth. Fear of loss, fear of missing out, fear of not being prepared (for the worst), fear that you won't be happy unless you have 'it' – all these fears are played upon in advertising tactics used to attack our sense of security and power. Ads for insurance, banking, health and fitness, medicines and medical equipment, the funeral industry, lottery tickets, - even household items - are all products and services where fear is the big trigger point for sales and marketing. Feeling bad enough already? How about trying the latest holiday destination, tastebud tempter, designer fashion trend, expensive toy the kids will love you for, or perfume that will make you soooo much more alluring to the opposite sex?

You get my drift. As I place my focus on understanding the meaning behind the CUSB Statements and apply them in my life, I become less concerned about the desire for the things that may bring me physical security and comfort. I feel safe and at peace within myself. The really cool thing is, as long as I remember that I have the power to create everything I need and want, it doesn't really matter what the advertisers throw at me. My desires, coupled with the appropriate action and self-belief, will always be met.

The Influence Of Action
The gooey mound of clay sits in front of us waiting to be moulded into something beautiful. We can stare at it all day, willing it to shape itself into the form we desire, but unless we actively involve ourselves in the process, our masterpiece will remain a gooey mound.

It seems to be contrary to Abraham's Three Step definition (see page 39), but there are actions we can take towards our goals that work with, rather than against, the Law of Attraction. Our mound of clay is a good example. We actually need to physically get involved with the clay, we need to get our hands dirty, to alter its shape and turn it into a vase.

When we have a desire for something, a goal we are aiming for, we have to assist the Universe, not work against it. Our thoughts have to be positive and in line with what we want (not with what we don't want – but we've already talked about that) and we have to place ourselves in a position of preparedness to receive our gift when the Universe is ready to deliver it.

We are powerful Beings filled with God Energy and we can achieve anything when we utilise the combined abilities that are unique to us as Humans. We have been given the built in tools of hands, feet and legs, brain and senses – a solid body with knowledge of how to use it - that allow us to create in physical form that which we imagine in our thoughts and crave in our spirit.

If you want to travel to India and sit on a mountaintop with a guru, place your request with The Universe and then open a holiday savings account, apply for your passport, do some research and start saving! The Universe will work with you in miraculous ways when you apply positive action as well as positive thought toward your desire, and you'll find yourself atop that mountain faster than you can say "Ohmmm".

I want to become a successful author. I want to write a book that helps others to reach their goals and find joy in their lives, but simply sending that desire out to The Universe isn't enough to make it happen. I must write the book and make it worthy of my readers. I have to research my publishing options and send out my manuscript to the Publishers I really want to work with. It's my job to work with joy, to promote and market my book. These are all the things that a successful author does so I do it with love. With positive energy via my thoughts, feelings and actions, and because I love what I'm doing, the Universe/God provides all that is necessary for my book to reach you. The energy that connects me to my book to the publishing industry to you, works in a co-operative way to deliver that which we have each asked for.

God Within
We are constantly creating. In every moment with every aspect of our Being, beginning with a thought, carried by our desire and brought forth through our action and belief, it is our nature to desire and create, desire and create, and then desire and create some more. It is our God-Self in constant desire of experiences and evolvement that urges us to keep creating in our life.

As perfectly synchronised Beings at one with the power of the Universe, the only barrier between God and us is the one we imagine into existence, the one we create for ourselves. On God's side of the equation there is no barrier and there never can be, because God cannot be separated from Itself. We are individual aspects of God and like a beautiful dance choreographed by the power we have within us, our God-Self resonates through the world.

Just like clay and Potter, we invent and reinvent, design and redesign, create and recreate as we reach out for perfection, without ever truly wanting to attain it. We enjoy our creative experience too much to stop – even if we could.

STATEMENT 16

Remain loving and joyful, for this is the deepest essence of Being.

I wish you abundance in all things...

I wish you abundance of the heart,
that it be filled with love
such as you've never known before.

I wish for you abundant wellbeing,
a healthy body and mind
and a life lived long and well.

I wish you abundance of the soul
and a knowing of your inner power
and of the beauty of God within you.

I wish you an abundance of joy
greater than any you've ever felt,
and lasting for an eternity.

I wish you the gift of abundant time
so that you may enjoy all that you are
and explore all that you want to be.

Most of all,
I wish for you abundant understanding
that you can have, be and do
anything your heart desires...

and live your dreams abundantly every day.

16

This Statement summarises the Constitution of the United States of Being perfectly, don't you think? It acts as a reminder to stay focused on our deepest truths;

- It is our inner most desire to live lovingly and joyfully.

- By our very nature, we are Love.

- We are irrevocably and exquisitely connected to each other and to all things.

- We exist to create and we create everything in our lives.

- We are perfect in our imperfection.

- We are infinite. We can never not be.

Though I feel the ring of these truths resonate deep within me, it's still a challenge to absorb them intellectually. I know that my Soul State sings when I focus on these truths therefore I will continue to throw myself passionately into their warm waters, so great is my desire to understand them - and the CUSB - fully. The big question is: How do we maintain all those positive 'warm and fuzzy' feelings when the world around us seems so chaotic and tumultuous? How do we remain loving and joyful when we are part of a society where hate, greed, fear and anger appear to be so much a part of it too?

The Unbreakable Bond

At the centre of our Being is the desire for connection. When we connect with others, we are connecting with other aspects of God - of ourselves. We thrive on relationships because they provide us with a variety of experiences from which we can create even more. It's not always easy, especially if the person you are connecting with is antagonistic and choosing to Be that which, in truth, they are not; in other words, if they are behaving in a manner that is contrary to loving and joyful. Okay, let's just say it: if they're being an ass!

It's just as important to recognise the well-hidden Highest Self of the antagonist who is challenging to us – perhaps more so – as it is to see a person's openly reflected Highest Self. In seeking to appreciate the authentic Being of love and light that is present in everyone (even when they're not demonstrating it), we are provided with the perfect opportunity for emotional and spiritual growth. From the point of view of the antagonist, they too, are given this opportunity. Regardless of the choices each makes, it's a win-win situation.

Relationship is all about creating experiences that allow us to make choices and reach for more: more experiences, more of what we desire and more opportunities to evolve. When we recognise and embrace the intrinsic beauty and perfection in every relationship and every experience, even those that challenge us, we fulfil our desire for love and joy – and peace – in our lives.

Feeling the connection to our Soul-Self is the core desire within each of us. We need more than the belief that we are merely several trillion impersonal cells linked together to create a finite bag of meat and bones with no long-term purpose or legacy to leave behind. Though we may not fully understand the mechanics of it, we know we are much more than merely physical. We feel the energy within and around us and the stirring in our heart and mind that calls forth a deep inner knowing that we are intrinsically connected to all things seen and unseen.

When we are in tune with all our States of Being - physical, emotional, spiritual and intellectual - we are living in balance with the Universe, the Source of All Things - God. I think one of the central themes of the CUSB is that no matter how disconnected we may feel at times, there is relief and peace to be found in knowing that the bond is unbreakable, for who can break God? Energy can be altered but it can never be destroyed or made non-existent, and neither can we. We are eternally bonded with, and part of, living Universal Force so any disconnection we feel is an illusion within our mind.

Blights to Blessings
We are born creators. It is the core of who we are as eternal Beings. It's our nature to create the experiences we need in order to evolve and expand, so it stands to reason that we are compelled to create seemingly adverse situations in our lives as a means to fulfil our mission. We all want stability and joy in our lives, and sure, serenity is wonderful, but without a counter-balance we would never know what to aim for. I believe turmoil gives us our greatest opportunity to thrive and evolve. Turmoil gives birth to our desire for peace and harmony, our desire for something more, something better.

In order to fully appreciate the emotions of love and compassion, we need to experience the lack of them. To appreciate great joy, we must also experience the feeling of deep sadness. Love would mean nothing to us if we were never to experience an opposing emotion like fear or hate. We are Beings of observation and perception, so in order to understand light, we must experience darkness.

Perhaps this is why the perception of turmoil is so important in our lives. When we experience something we don't like, it gives us the opportunity to change it, to choose differently.

All those dramas that rise to meet us, from the daily challenges in our individual lives to the global issues that affect us as part of the human community, are designed to compel us to make choices. Choices in the way we think and the actions we take to inspire growth and evolvement.

We have no authority over our past. Whilst we can choose the way we feel about our past, we cannot change or undo it. We do, however, have power over our present and our future by way of the personal choices we begin to make right now. Our future will become our present and our present will become our past, so by choosing to live joyfully and lovingly now we are creating a past we can look back on with pleasure rather than pain.

If there's one thing of which I am certain, it's that we each have the ability to change the world in a beautiful, profound and permanent way. And therein lays the answer. When we can view hate, greed, anger and fear (or any other negative thought, word or action) as a means by which we can make a change and create something different, it stops being a blight on our life and instead becomes a blessing. We are given the opportunity to observe the various options available and define our preferences.

Our Perfect Imperfection
There are some situations and challenges that have the capacity to knock us right off our perch. It happens to all of us, and berating ourselves when we are feeling less than loving and joyful only makes matters worse. We are Beings existing in a physical Human State which means we are designed to feel every emotion on the spectrum. The key to getting through the challenging moments is to be gentle with ourselves, acknowledge how we are feeling and why, and, with the help of the CUSB, work our way back to a positive mental and emotional space.

When I have a flash of anger or I feel really upset about something that's occurred, I make myself stop, step back and breathe. I put space between me and whatever has set me off, allowing time to work through my processes and find my balance again. It used to take a long time to get from the negative place to the positive one – sometimes weeks and even months – but these days, it's rare for me to sit in my emotional muck for more than a few hours. Mostly, I work my way up to feeling better within a few minutes. That doesn't mean that I can go from seething to 'sweetness-and-light' in every situation, but it works for most of them. It can be that way for you too.

That's the great thing about being perfectly imperfect. We are not just going through the process of life. We are the process; perpetual in nature, constantly in motion and with infinite choices available to us. We can't always control the situation, but we can control how we choose to experience it emotionally and psychologically. Reminded of this, we can be instantly calmed and strengthened even in the deepest of crises. We can choose the way we think, feel and react in any situation. We have that power.

We make mistakes. That's part of Being Human. As they say, "build a bridge and get over it". We don't always perform the gestures of love and joy we are capable of, but just knowing we have the capacity for greatness is enough to compel us forward to reach for those highest aspects of ourselves. So be gentle on yourself and others, forgive the mistakes and move on. Remember that we are imperfectly perfect and that's the way we're meant to be.

Being Eternal
We exist as many States of Being simultaneously; physical, emotional, spiritual and intellectual - mind, body, soul. We are pure, living energy. As non-physical, Soul Beings, we are constant and infinite, powerful and creative. There is no means by which we cannot exist as part of Universal Force.

We are part of All That Is, with no beginning and no end. Our physical body is finite and will eventually cease to exist, but our thoughts, feelings, words and actions, once created, cannot be un-created. These are the eternal aspects of our physical State.

I think that's why this Statement is more than simply a wrap-up of the others. More than a conclusion, it is a Soul-deep mantra that resonates through the eternal God Energy that connects us - that is us. Regardless of our Human goals and dreams, when we look for the core desire to everything we want, it is to live in a State of love and joy.
Everything we think, feel, say and do comes from a place of love and/or joy – or the lack of it – in our life. We can't really get it 'wrong' and we have all of eternity to experience everything the Universe has on offer and everything we continue to create. Of course, the sooner we consciously choose to seek out that which makes us feel good and inspires love and joy within us, the sooner we can really start to enjoy the journey. Either way, as physical individuals and as Universal God Force, we learn, grow, evolve and become 'more' with each experience.

This extraordinary Human life of both physical and non-physical energetic existence is like a fabulous, never-ending rollercoaster ride. Created with ups, downs, twists and turns, it's safe but scary and always exhilarating. The way you experience it depends on whether you choose to laugh your way through it with joyful abandon or close your eyes and scream. Neither choice is wrong but I love a good rollercoaster so I know which choice I'll continue to make. ☺

***

Writing this book has been a revelation to me. My understanding of the Constitution of the United States of Being has expanded a thousand-fold. My understanding of my Self has grown even more. The act of writing down the processes that I use, and contemplating more thoroughly my ideas and beliefs surrounding the Statements, has birthed in me a deeper desire to abide by their loving advice. I thought I was well on the way but, since beginning this literary journey, I find myself living in even greater States of appreciation, abundance, forgiveness and joy. So, I know that if nothing else, writing this book has caused me to grow and evolve into an even better version of imperfect perfection.

We live in a time of great spiritual and intellectual enlightenment. We are beginning to understand that whatever we create in this world is a testament, not only of our level of evolvement as Humans Being, but also of our understanding of the connection we have to All That Is. The Constitutional Statements lovingly advise us how to thrive within ourselves and how to become inspiring beacons of light, love, hope and creativity in the lives of others. When we choose to live accordingly, we truly are living as beautifully balanced, perfectly imperfect, joyfully loving, United States of Being.

GUIDELINES FOR A SUCCESSFUL LIFE (1998)

1. Believe wholeheartedly in your Hopes and your Dreams.

2. Have faith in yourself.

3. Develop your Inner Power and Instincts.

4. Stand up to your fears – they cannot harm you unless you allow them to.

5. Replace your fear of the unknown with trust in yourself.

6. Anger and resentment are the two most negative and destructive emotions – learn to live without them.

7. Be loving and kind to yourself and you will find it easier to be loving and kind to others.

8. You can have/do/be anything you desire – if you desire it enough.

9. You and you alone are responsible for your actions.

The Constitution of the United States of Being

10. You can never make a wrong choice. There are good choices and bad choices, but all choices lead us to another learning experience.

11. When you find your life's path, don't be afraid to step off it occasionally. There is much beauty to be found on the side of the road, and new experiences to discover. Often the lessons on these side journeys help us further 'down the track'.

12. You can change yourself, but you cannot change other people.

13. You can lead, but you cannot force others to follow.

14. The love, respect and friendship of others must be earned. To receive these three things is a privilege, not a right.

15. Above all else, learn to love who you are. Learn to enjoy your 'Self' and be excited about the life you've been given.

16. You are both the clay and the Potter. Delight in your changes, growth and Power.

17. Remain a Loving Being.

ACKNOWLEDGEMENTS

To my awesome son, Mason: Thank you for coming into my life. There is no one I love more.

To my mother, Doreen, and my father, Stan: You both mean the world to me. Thanks for teaching me so much over the years and for your love and support. You can never know how much it means to me.

To my sister, Christine, the most amazing person I know: I love and appreciate everything about you.

To Chris Headford: Thank you for being such a wonderful father to our son and friend to me - and for being a fabulous webmaster. Wattlegum Web Works rocks!!

A huge "thank you" and a mountain of love to Debbie Benson, Andrea Szabo, Toni Koch, Jason Blume, Alan Roy Scott, Diana Torossian, Rusty Wallis, Jane Robertson, Gilli Moon, Eliza Warner, and Jerry Altavilla for your incredible love and support over the years as I've reached for my dreams.

A special thanks and loads of love to all my 'ASCers', especially Michael Kuchera, Terri Rowe, Kerrie Garside, Karen Anne Waters, Derick Jason, Rhubee Neale, Rochelle Swift, Karise Higgins, Nick Roberts, Kathy Prosser, Susan Muranty,

Alexandra Jae, Elizabeth Usher, Lola Brinton and Trisha Rolan for sharing your special gifts of talent, love and support.

My deepest appreciation for help with the editing, feedback and general saving of my sanity during the writing of this book goes to Toni Koch, Liz Macnamara, Clem Gorman, my writing peers and champions of The Half-Written Book Club at Woy Woy, and the dozens of wonderful people who 'test-read' the manuscript including Kirsten Basilotta, Ric Bennett, Christina Burke, Merelyn Carter, Meaghan Clark, Mary Harrison, Rachel Hawkins, Nicole Mottlee, Terry Shepherd, Vern Ward, Laurie Williams and Monica Wright all of whom offered their feedback to make the book stronger.

My very special thanks to the following people whose financial contributions helped to make this book a published reality: Mary Harrison, Susan Muranty, Elizabeth Usher, Vern Ward, and Doreen Van Bree.

To all the awesome staff of Ruby's Cafe & Books at Umina Beach, especially Kirsten, thank you for letting me take up space and thanks for the much-appreciated constant stream of fabulous lattes that kept me going so I could finish this book!

A heart-felt "thank you" and deepest appreciation to the great teachers who I've never met but whose work has inspired me over the years: Richard Bach, Neale Donald Walsch, Abraham, Louise Hay, Jesus Christ, Deepak Chopra, Colin Tipping, Cheryl Richardson and Marci Shimoff, to name but a few.

And finally, to you, the reader of this book, thank you for sharing this amazing journey of Life with me. Thank you for everything you are and all you desire to be. I wish you love, joy and abundance as you continue to create, experience and evolve as an individual and as part of Universal Force/God/All That Is. You are a beautiful gift to the planet and our Oneness brings me great joy. I appreciate you.

ABOUT THE AUTHOR

Lisa J. Butler has always had a pen in her hand. She wrote poetry as a child and turned to song writing in her teens, eventually winding up in the music industry as a coach and consultant.

A Life, Career & Motivational Coach, Lisa assists her clients to define their goals and overcome their personal roadblocks through coaching sessions, workshops and seminars – all based on the principles of the CUSB statements. Her coaching and seminar service is aptly named 'Joyful and Free'.

An accomplished poet, a number of Lisa's poems appear on cards and in book anthologies through Blue Mountain Press, the Colorado-based international publishing company.

Lisa runs music career workshops and song writer seminars, and she coaches talented performing artists, songwriters and musicians in craft and career through Lisa Butler Music Consulting. Lisa is founder and organiser of the Australian Songwriters Conference.

A single mother of one young son who attends primary school, Lisa resides in Woy Woy on the Central Coast of New South Wales, Australia.

The Constitution of the United States of Being is Lisa's first book.

Contact

Email: mail@lisajbutler.com
Post: PO Box 122, Woy Woy, NSW 2256 Australia

Website: www.lisajbutler.com
Facebook: Lisa J. Butler (LyricaLisa)

www.ingramcontent.com/pod-product-compliance
Lightning Source LLC
LaVergne TN
LVHW051558070426
835507LV00021B/2635